CONTENTS

GENERAL EDITOR'S PREFACE

The aim of the Macmillan Master Guides is to help you to appreciate the book you are studying by providing information about it and by suggesting ways of reading and thinking about it which will lead to a fuller understanding. The section on the writer's life and background has been designed to illustrate those aspects of the writer's life which have influenced the work, and to place it in its personal and literary context. The summaries and critical commentary are of special importance in that each brief summary of the action is followed by an examination of the significant critical points. The space which might have been given to repetitive explanatory notes has been devoted to a detailed analysis of the kind of passage which might confront you in an examination. Literary criticism is concerned with both the broader aspects of the work being studied and with its detail. The ideas which meet us in reading a great work of literature, and their relevance to us today, are an essential part of our study, and our Guides look at the thought of their subject in some detail. But just as essential is the craft with which the writer has constructed his work of art, and this may be considered under several technical headings — characterisation, language, style and stagecraft, for example.

The authors of these Guides are all teachers and writers of wide experience, and they have chosen to write about books they admire and know well in the belief that they can communicate their admiration to you. But you yourself must read and know intimately the book you are studying. No one can do that for you. You should see this book as a lamp-post. Use it to shed light, not to lean against. If you know your text and know what it is saying about life, and how it says it, then you will enjoy it, and there is no better way of passing an examination in literature.

JAMES GIBSON

MACMILLAN MASTER GUIDES
THE MERCHANT OF VENICE
BY WILLIAM SHAKESPEARE

A. M. KINGHORN

with an Introduction by
HAROLD BROOKS

MACMILLAN

First published 1988 by
MACMILLAN PRESS LTD
Houndmills, Basingstoke, Hampshire RG21 6XS
and London
Companies and representatives
throughout the world

ISBN 0-333-44251-2

A catalogue record for this book is available
from the British Library.

12 11 10 9 8 7 6 5 4
04 03 02 01 00 99 98 97 96

Printed in Malaysia

AN INTRODUCTION TO THE STUDY OF SHAKESPEARE'S PLAYS

A play as a work of art exists to the full only when performed. It must hold the audience's attention throughout the performance, and, unlike a novel, it can't be put down and taken up again. It is important to experience the play as if you are seeing it on the stage for the first time, and you should begin by reading it straight through. Shakespeare builds a play in dramatic units which may be divided into smaller subdivisions, or episodes, markcd off by exits and entrances and lasting as long as the same actors are on the stage. Study it unit by unit.

The first unit provides the exposition which is designed to put the audience into the picture. In the second unit we see the forward movement of the play as one situation changes into another. The last unit in a tragedy or a tragical play will bring the catastrophe, and in comedy — and some of the history plays — an unravelling of the complications, what is called a *dénouement*.

The onward movement of the play from start to finish is its progressive structure. We see the chain of cause and effect (the plot) and the progressive revelation and development of character. The people, their characters and their motives drive the plot forward in a series of scenes which are carefully planned to give variety of pace and excitement. We notice fast-moving and slower-moving episodes, tension mounting and slackening, and alternative fear and hope for the characters we favour. Full-stage scenes, such as stately councils and processions or turbulent mobs, contrast with scenes of small groups or even single speakers. Each of the scenes presents a deed or event which changes the situation. In performances, entrances and exits and stage actions are physical facts, with more impact than on the page. That impact Shakespeare relied upon, and we must restore it by an effort of the imagination.

Shakespeare's language is just as diverse. Quickfire dialogue is followed by long speeches, and verse changes to prose. There is a wide range of speech — formal, colloquial, dialect, 'Mummerset' and the broken English of foreigners, for example. Songs, instrumental music, and the noise of battle, revelry and tempest, all extend the range of dramatic expression. The dramatic use of language is enhanced by skilful stagecraft, by costumes, by properties such as beds, swords and Yorick's skull, by such stage business as kneeling, embracing and giving money, and by use of such features of the stage structure as the balcony and the trapdoor.

By these means Shakespeare's people are brought vividly to life and cleverly individualised. But though they have much to tell us about human nature, we must never forget that they are characters in a play, not in real life. And remember, they exist to enact the play, not the play to portray *them*.

Shakespeare groups his characters so that they form a pattern, and it is useful to draw a diagram showing this. Sometimes a linking character has dealings with each group. The pattern of persons belongs to the symmetric structure of the play, and its dramatic unity is reinforced and enriched by a pattern of resemblances and contrasts; for instance, between characters, scenes, recurrent kinds of imagery, and words. It is not enough just to notice a feature that belongs to the symmetric structure, you should ask what its relevance is to the play as a whole and to the play's ideas.

These ideas and the dramatising of them in a central theme, or several related to each other, are a principal source of the dramatic unity. In order to see what themes are present and important, look, as before, for pattern. Observe the place in it of the leading character. In tragedy this will be the protagonist, in comedy heroes and heroines, together with those in conflict or contrast with them. In *Henry IV Part I,* Prince Hal is being educated for kingship and has a correct estimate of honour, while Falstaff despises honour, and Hotspur makes an idol of it. Pick out the episodes of great intensity as, for example, in *King Lear* where the theme of spiritual blindness is objectified in the blinding of Gloucester, and similarly, note the emphases given by dramatic poetry as in Prospero's 'Our revels now are ended . . .'or unforgettable utterances such as Lear's 'Is there any cause in Nature that makes these hard hearts?' Striking stage-pictures such as that of Hamlet behind the King at prayer will point to leading themes, as will all the parallels and recurrences, including those of phrase and imagery. See whether, in the play you are studying, themes known to be favourites with Shakespeare are prominent, themes such as those of order and dis-order, relationships disrupted by mistakes about identity, and appearance and reality. The latter were bound to fascinate Shakespeare, whose theatrical art worked by means of illusions which pointed beyond the surface of actual life to underlying truths. In looking at themes beware of attempts to make the play fit some orthodoxy a critic believes in — Freudian perhaps, or Marxist, or dogmatic Christian theology — and remember that its ideas, though they often have a bearing on ours, are Elizabethan.

Some of Shakespeare's greatness lies in the good parts he wrote for the actors. In his demands upon them, and the opportunities he provided, he bore their professional skills in mind and made use of their physical prowess, relished by a public accustomed to judge fencing and wrestling as expertly as we today judge football and tennis. As a member of the professional group of players called The Chamberlain's Men he knew each actor he was writing for. To play his women he had highly trained boys. As paired heroines they were often contrasted, short with tall, for example, or one vivacious and enterprising, the other more conventionally feminine.

Richard Burbage, the company's leading man, was famous as a great tragic actor, and he took leading roles in seven of Shakespeare's *tragedies*. Though each of the seven has its own distinctiveness, we shall find at the centre of all of them a tragic protagonist possessing tragic greatness, not just one 'tragic flaw' but a tragic vulnerability. He will have a character which makes him unfit to cope with the tragic situations confronting him, so that his tragic errors bring down upon him tragic suffering and finally a tragic catastrophe. Normally, both the suffering and the catastrophe are far worse than he can be said to deserve, and others are engulfed in them who deserve such a fate less or not at all. Tragic terror is aroused in us because, though exceptional, he is sufficiently near to normal humankind for his fate to remind us of what can happen to human beings like ourselves, and because we see in it a combination of inexorable law and painful mystery. We recognise the principle of cause and effect where in a tragic world errors return upon those who make them, but we are also aware of the tragic disproportion between cause and effect. In a tragic world you may kick a stone and start an avalanche which will destroy you and others with you. Tragic pity is aroused in us by this disproportionate suffering, and also by all the kinds of suffering undergone by every character who has won our imaginative sympathy. Imaginative sympathy is wider than moral approval, and is felt even if suffering does seem a just and logical outcome. In addition to pity and terror we have a sense of tragic waste because catastrophe has affected so much that was great and fine. Yet we feel also a tragic exaltation. To our grief the men and women who represented those values have been destroyed, but the values themselves have been shown not to depend upon success, nor upon immunity from the worst of tragic sufferings and disaster.

Comedies have been of two main kinds, or cross-bred from the two. In critical comedies the governing aim is to bring out the absurdity or irrationality of follies and abuses, and make us laugh at them. Shakespeare's comedies often do this, but most of them belong primarily to the other kind – romantic comedy. Part of the romantic appeal is to our liking for suspense; they are dramas of averted threat, beginning in trouble and ending in joy. They appeal to the romantic senses of adventure and of wonder, and to complain that they are improbable is silly because the improbability, the marvellousness, is part of the pleasure. They dramatise stories of romantic love, accompanied by love doctrine – ideas and ideals of love. But they are plays in two tones, they are comic as well as romantic. There is often something to laugh at even in the love stories of the nobility and gentry, and just as there is high comedy in such incidents as the cross-purposes of the young Athenians in the wood, and Rosalind as 'Ganymede' teasing Orlando, there is always broad comedy for characters of lower rank. Even where one of the sub-plots has no effect on the main plot, it may take up a topic from it and present it in a more comic way.

What is there in the play to make us laugh or smile? We can distinguish many kinds of comedy it may employ. *Language* can amuse by its wit, or by absurdity, as in Bottom's malapropisms. Feste's nonsense-phrases, so fatuously admired by Sir Andrew, are deliberate, while his catechising of Olivia is clown-routine. Ass-headed Bottom embraced by the Fairy Queen is a *comic spectacle* combining costume and stage-business. His wanting to play every part is *comedy of character*. Phebe disdaining Silvius and in love with 'Ganymede', or Malvolio treating Olivia as though she had written him a love-letter is *comedy of situation*; the situation is laughably different from what Phebe or Malvolio supposes. A comic let-down or anticlimax can be devastating, as we see when Arragon, sure that he deserves Portia, chooses the silver casket only to find the portrait not of her but of a 'blinking idiot'. By *slapstick, caricature* or sheer *ridiculousness of situation*, comedy can be exaggerated into farce, which Shakespeare knows how to use on occasion. At the opposite extreme, before he averts the threat, he can carry it to the brink of tragedy, but always under control.

Dramatic irony is the result of a character or the audience anticipating an outcome which, comically or tragically, turns out very differently. Sometimes *we* foresee that it will. The speaker never foresees how ironical, looking back, the words or expectations will appear. When she says, 'A little water clears us of this deed,' Lady Macbeth has no prevision of her sleep-walking words, 'Will these hands ne'er be clean?' There is irony in the way in which in all Shakespeare's tragic plays except *Richard II* comedy is found in the very heart of the tragedy. The Porter scene in *Macbeth* comes straight after Duncan's murder. In *Hamlet* and *Antony and Cleopatra* comic episodes lead into the catastrophe: the rustic Countryman brings Cleopatra the means of death, and the satirised Osric departs with Hamlet's assent to the fatal fencing match. The Porter, the Countryman and Osric are not mere 'comic relief', they contrast with the tragedy in a way that adds something to it, and affects our response.

A sense of the comic and the tragic is common ground between Shakespeare and his audience. Understandings shared with the audience are necessary to all drama. They include conventions, i.e. assumptions, contrary to what factual realism would demand, which the audience silently agrees to accept. It is, after all, by a convention, what Coleridge called a 'willing suspension of disbelief', that an actor is accepted as Hamlet. We should let a play teach us the conventions it depends on. Shakespeare's conventions allow him to take a good many liberties, and he never troubles about inconsistencies that wouldn't trouble an audience. What matters to the dramatist is the effect he creates. So long as we are responding as he would wish, Shakespeare would not care whether we could say by what means he has made us do so. But to appreciate his skill, and get a fuller understanding of his play, we have to distinguish these means, and find terms to describe them.

If you approach the Shakespeare play you are studying bearing in mind what is said to you here, then you will respond to it more fully than before. Yet like all works of artistic genius, Shakespeare's can only be analysed so far. His drama and its poetry will always have about them something 'which into words no critic can digest'.

HAROLD BROOKS

ACKNOWLEDGEMENTS

Text: All quotations from and textual references to *The Merchant of Venice* relate to the edition by Christopher Parry (London: Macmillan, 1985). Highly recommended is the Arden edition, edited by John Russell Brown (London: Methuen, 1977), which has a detailed introduction.

Cover illustration: *The Trial Scene* by R. Smirke, from the RSC Collection, with permission of the Governors of the Royal Shakespeare Theatre.

1 SHAKESPEARE'S LIFE

Shakespeare's biography is partly hidden in the mists of anonymity. It is based on parish registers, baptismal and marriage certificates, his own last will and testament, contemporary references, local traditions (mainly unsupported by solid fact) and what personal revelations may be drawn from the plays themselves. Written record is the most reliable but the least informative about the man who created Antonio, Bassanio, Portia, Shylock and the other characters who bring the text of *The Merchant of Venice* to life on the modern stage. Shakespeare lives through his works and the fact that his life story is what the Italian philosopher-critic, Benedetto Croce, called *lacunosa* (tending to patchiness and full of blank spaces), is of secondary importance.

We know something of his forebears. His father was John Shakespeare, his mother Mary, *née* Arden, both natives of Stratford-upon-Avon in Warwickshire. John Shakespeare started as a trader in leather goods and over the years rose to a highly respected position in Stratford, reaching the office of High Bailiff, corresponding to mayor of the town. One of his posts was that of Town Constable, like the character Dogberry in *Much Ado About Nothing*. Shakespeare senior was rewarded with a coat of arms which his eldest son William inherited. He died in 1601, but Mary lived on until 1609 to witness the rise of her eldest son to fame and fortune.

William, baptised on 26 April 1564, is stated to have been born on 23 April, celebrated as St George's Day. He had two elder sisters, Joan and Margaret. 1564 was a plague year in Stratford with over two hundred deaths recorded but none of the Shakespeares succumbed. Between then and 1569 three boys and two girls were born into the family, making eight children in all.

Tradition places William in the King's New School, Stratford Grammar, where he followed the standard curriculum, which included Latin, some Greek, the Scriptures and Arithmetic. From his plays one may conclude that he did not enjoy his schooldays and from his contemporary Ben Jonson that he was no classical scholar, though the opinions of other playwrights may have been inspired by envy and must be judged accordingly. Other 'traditions' make him a school-master, a lawyer, a sailor, a soldier, a poacher and even a holder of gentlemen's horses outside the one and only London theatre. The last two may be connected, since if he did poach Sir Thomas Lucy's deer (an unlikely but persistent tale) it is not surprising that he found it expedient to leave the locales of his youth and go up to London to seek his fortune, arriving there in about 1587.

In 1582, aged eighteen, he had married Anne Hathaway, a local girl eight years his senior. She bore him a daughter five months afterwards and, two years later, twins, Hamnet and Judith. Hamnet died in 1596, shortly before his father's greatest dramatic successes, known as his 'tragic' period. Apart from these few authenticated facts, hardly anything is known about Shakespeare's life between marriage and his emergence as a successful dramatist in London, hence the rich growth of legend to fill the gap in continuity. Scholars, like nature, abhor a vacuum.

Shakespeare must have seen the mediaeval miracle plays in Stratford before they were banned as 'papist', and been entertained by troupes of strolling players – one is known to have visited the town in 1587. Otherwise, we know nothing of how he came to be stage-struck, but in London he achieved success. Soon he acquired a patron, essential for advancement in those days. This gentleman was the Third Earl of Southampton, to whom he dedicated two narrative poems, *Venus and Adonis* and *The Rape of Lucrece*. Before 1592 he wrote *Henry VI* in three parts, followed by a string of comedies, including *Love's Labour's Lost* and *The Comedy of Errors*, distingu-ished by an ebullience of language and indulgence in figurative speech, extravagant metaphors and rhetorical control which set him above all his contemporaries except Christopher Marlowe, from whose example he obviously learned much.

From his father Shakespeare seems to have inherited a natural business acumen. His first plays were performed in 'The Theatre' in Finsbury Fields, Shoreditch, outside the city walls. This was the very first public theatre to be built for that purpose, by James Burbage whose son Richard became a lifelong associate of Shakespeare's and is celebrated as the first actor known to have played Hamlet. Shakespeare himself purchased an interest in an acting troupe called The Chamberlain's Men and acquired a holding in the Globe Theatre, Southwark, on the river bank.

When the lease of Burbage's theatre expired it was transported across the Thames to become the (new) Globe, with a thatched roof. To Shakespeare's time at the Globe belong the four great tragedies, starting with *Hamlet* (1600). Shakespeare is said to have played minor or walk-on roles, including those of the Ghost in *Hamlet*, Adam in *As You Like It* and Time in *The Winter's Tale*. *The Merchant of Venice* offers several such roles – Bassanio's or Portia's servants, for example. He became what is now called an actor–manager and the playing of such parts enabled him to supervise production during most of the performance. In fact, the backstage warning 'the ghost walks' is supposed to have originated in the days when Shakespeare, having made his appearances on the Elsinore battlements, went round to collect the day's takings.

In 1601 his patron Southampton was sentenced to life imprisonment for his involvement with the Earl of Essex's rebellion, but by this time Shakespeare had become well known and enjoyed royal patronage. In 1608 he shared the lease of the Blackfriars' Theatre, with a roof to shelter the actors. He had become prosperous, owning dwellings, pastures and arable land in his native Stratford, but there is no record of his ever having acquired property in London and he probably lived in lodgings. His capital had been built up from actor-management rather than from writing for the stage and his attitude to his art was undoubtedly that of the professional who gave his audience what he knew they wanted, including social and political commentary. So far as we know, he never travelled abroad and his foreign settings are products of his imagination, though no doubt he listened to returning travellers.

In about 1610–11 Shakespeare left London and retired to his native Stratford for the years remaining to him. His latest group of plays, the romantic comedies, concluded with *The Tempest* in 1611. Coincidentally, in his end was his beginning, for Shakespeare died on St George's Day, 1616 and his last work, *The Tempest*, was printed first in order in the earliest printed edition of the plays. Shakespeare had written at least thirty-six of them and assisted in the writing of others, including *Henry VIII* in this final group. The exact order of their composition is not known for certain, but *The Merchant of Venice* was probably about his twelfth play, conceived not earlier than 1594. By then he had managed to eliminate the rhetorical excesses of the earlier comedies and rough edges of the earlier tragedies and had improved his technique in matching words to action, thus creating true 'poetic' drama, aided by better staging facilities.

His death is shrouded in mystery. Did he really die from a fever after drinking with Ben Jonson? Did the plague strike Stratford again and carry him off? His last will, legally autographed, bequeathed his 'second-best bed' (the best one was normally reserved for visitors) to his wife Anne. He was interred in the local parish church of the Holy Trinity, where he had been baptised fifty-two years before and Anne placed a bust of her husband in the niche above his grave, accompanied by a sinister admonitory epitaph:

> Good friend for Jesus sake forbeare
> To digg the dust enclosed heare
> Blest be the Man that spares the Stones
> And curst be he that moves my bones

Anne herself died in 1623. In that same year two of the surviving Chamberlain's Men had all Shakespeare's plays printed in a single volume, known as the First Folio. No authentic manuscripts survive and the poet's own handwriting is represented only by signatures on legal documents. The same compilers commissioned a Flemish engraver, Martin Droeshout, to create a frontispiece portrait, but this young man could never have met his subject and the result, perhaps based on the Stratford bust, is uninspired. More to be relied upon is the anonymous portrait named after one of its owners, Lord Chandos, but formerly in the possession of Sir William Davenant, Shakespeare's godson. The Droeshout and Chandos likenesses have some features in common and the many hundreds of pictures painted since that time all show the same type of round visage, high domed forehead, receding hair and intense gaze: not, one might conclude, the face of a genius, but all we have left to suggest what England's greatest dramatist looked like.

2 THE HISTORICAL
BACKGROUND OF THE PLAY

2.1 SHAKESPEARE AND TRADITIONS OF ANTI-SEMITISM

The Merchant of Venice has lost none of its force with the passage of time. The central character is immediately identifiable by appearance, speech and manner as a member of an alien race, representing a minority-group culture and religion. However, Shakespeare did not conceive this play in order to advance our modern cause of racial equality. The Elizabethans were not noted for their tolerance.

Persecutions of Jews, sanctioned officially, are chronicled in early documents of the Christian Church. Repressive acts against them were first recorded in the fourth century AD and John Chrysostom's eight sermons of 397 provided generations of later writers with material for anti-semitic diatribes. Chrysostom described Jews as sensual, obscene, daemonic, money-making, accursed devil-worshipping murderers of the Prophets, of Christ and of God, and called them drunkards, whoremongers, and criminals. The synagogue he denounced as a whorehouse, den of iniquity, pandemonium or house of Satan, soul-destroying habitation and yawning abyss of perdition. Other early church documents are laced with similarly abusive language, justifying rejection of the Jews on the ground that they had been disinherited by God. Forced mass-baptism was practised in the sixth century under the Emperor Justinian.

Edward I, heavily in debt to Jewish money-lenders, solved his economic problems by expelling them, and in Shakespeare's time Jews were still not permitted to live in England unless they volunteered to go through the ancient baptismal ritual of conversion to Christianity. In the 1570s Joachim Gaunz, a Jewish mining expert from Prague working in Bristol, was denounced, arrested, sent to London and, by order of the Privy Council, deported because he refused conversion. This was the normal application of Edward's thirteen-century statute (later repealed by Oliver Cromwell). However, a converted Jew was usually left alone provided that he did not draw attention to himself and there was a home for converts in Chancery Lane. They tended to dwell together for mutual security, to maintain strong family relationships and not to mix with Gentiles. Although they practised a variety of trades, Jews were known mainly as usurers who lent money at interest, then, and perhaps even now, a despised occupation when individuals rather than banks engage in it.

The Elizabethan citizen, brought up on a traditional orthodox Christian distaste for usury, regarded it as a sin, even though the legal rate of interest at that time was fixed at ten per cent and bankers from the Royal Exchange like Sir Thomas Gresham were trying to borrow on Queen Elizabeth's uncertain credit in Antwerp's money-markets. The English aristocracy from the Queen downwards, and including Shakespeare's patron Southampton, were heavily in debt and Sir Francis Bacon's 1625 essay *Of Usury* stated realistically that it was 'inevitable'. Nevertheless, hypocritical official postures condemned this expanding practice and Shakespeare, through his cartoon of this Jewish money-lender on whom two Christians are forced to rely, is certainly making a social and political comment to be interpreted as his audience wished.

Shylock is the Jew of Venice, a noted commercial port, at that time one of the richest trading cities in the world. Its population included wealthy citizens who gained and lost vast sums on the Rialto, the Venetian Stock Exchange. In such a milieu usury was necessary. On a less ambitious scale, the same activity went on in London. A contemporary writer of plays, Stephen Gosson, praised Marlowe's *The Jew of Malta* for its attack on usury, but Shakespeare, drawing on popular sentiment and official 'moral' postures, was still ready to present both sides of an argument, and gave Shylock the right words to justify this practice.

To put one of these rejected people into a stage play was not original to Shakespeare. Jewish characters had appeared in other plays, usually as stock villains deriving from the personification of Vice in mediaeval morality plays. His contemporary Marlowe's Barabas in *The Jew of Malta* falls into this category. Barabas embodied the Elizabethan playgoer's idea of a human type whom he had never met but only heard about as a mean, heartless, anti-Christian devil incarnate. Shylock is several times referred to as a 'devil' but, though he is cast in the same mould, he represents a marked advance on Marlowe's stereotyped creation.

The Elizabethan stage Jew was a creature of exotic reputation rather than of personal acquaintance but it was widely believed that he hated Christians and would go to any extreme to harm them. The model was mediaeval Christian tradition, not some live London example. Moreover it was at that time unthinkable that a Jew should try to hit back at his persecutors, yet this is what Shylock is made to do. Shakespeare shows with great originality of conception that his passions might in human terms be considered in a sympathetic light. The playwright can never be associated with any particular religion, cause or ideology, though in general it may be deduced from the plays that he subscribed to the prevailing belief that the universe was regulated and that human society should strive to reflect the same order.

2.2 PATERNAL AUTHORITY

In Venetian society paternal authority, supported by civil and canon law, was sacrosanct and to defy it required courage. Such defiance risked severe punishment, even including death, which under certain circumstances was a father's prerogative, though such an extreme penalty was rarely exacted in practice. Disobedient sons were usually disinherited or exiled, fallen daughters locked away or despatched to convents. Heavy paternalism was not uncommon in Europe and, though the English were not nearly so strict, they agreed that a father's authority ought to be upheld.

The Merchant of Venice dramatises what for an English audience was an unfamiliar example of a daughter's wilful rejection of her father's authority, since in this instance the family is orthodox Jewish. Jessica's conduct appears to have some justification, since Shylock is depicted as a domestic tyrant of the old school who frustrates his child's natural desires and does nothing to please her at home. She repays him by robbing him and eloping with a Christian, even becoming converted herself. From the point of view of the Jewish community this was the worst possible disaster that could befall an orthodox Jewish family and in such a case the girl would be struck from their memory and even regarded as dead. Shylock's growl at III.i 93–4 that he would prefer Jessica dead and buried along with the ducats she stole from him is realistic. This detail shows how well Shakespeare understood the subjects of his portrayals, even when they were remote from his own and his audience's immediate experience.

2.3 REFERENCES TO CONTEMPORARY EVENTS

It is never safe to assume that Shakespeare was inspired directly by history, though he undoubtedly used topical material when it suited his purpose. *The Merchant* has been related to the execution of a Portuguese Jew, Roderigo Lopéz, in 1594. Lopéz, a Christian convert, was denounced and hounded to the scaffold as an attempted poisoner of the Queen, an offence of which he was almost certainly guiltless. Marlowe's *The Jew of Malta* was probably inspired by the

Lopéz affair but apart from an association with *lupus*, the Latin word for wolf (IV.i.133–7), there is no conclusive allusion in *The Merchant*. Presumably the heightened anti-semitism of the time, and the outbreak in London of anti-foreign riots between 1588 (the year of the Spanish Armada) and 1595 encouraged Shakespeare to create his own Jewish character, though both the pound of flesh and the casket plots were well known and an earlier lost play, *The Jew*, of unknown authorship, dealt with usury.

Salerio's reference at I.i.27 to 'my wealthy Andrew docked in sand' probably alludes to a large Spanish galleon, named 'St Andrew', captured after she ran aground at Cadiz in July, 1596 and brought to England a month later. This may suggest the earliest date for the play's composition.

3 SUMMARIES AND CRITICAL COMMENTARIES

3.1 SYNOPSIS OF THE PLOT

'Plot' is sometimes confused with 'action' but refers here to a consecutive account of the events in the play separated from their meaning.

The play opens on a street in Venice. The 'merchant' of the story is Antonio, sad without knowing why. Bassanio, a bachelor friend, with two other young men, Gratiano and Lorenzo, tries unsuccessfully to cheer him up. Bassanio confides in Antonio, saying he wants to marry a rich heiress of Belmont, the beautiful Portia, but is short of the money he needs to make the sea voyage to her palace and compete on level terms with princely suitors. Antonio is willing to lend Bassanio the money but has no ready cash as all his fortune is tied up at sea, with cargoes despatched on trade routes to various parts of the world. However he assures Bassanio that he will stand surety for a loan from a source in Venice if Bassanio will make the necessary enquiries.

In Venice we also encounter Shylock, a Jewish money-lender, who hates Antonio (1) because he is a Christian, (2) because Shylock, a Jew, has endured racial insults from him and (3) because the merchant, unlike Shylock, makes loans interest-free, thus under-cutting the Jew's business. This last item particularly incenses him. Shylock agrees to lend Bassanio the money but, after deliberating, imposes an unusual condition on Antonio, introduced half-humorously, to the effect that failure to repay the loan within a three-month grace period will give Shylock the right to cut a pound of flesh from whatever part of Antonio's body he wishes.

In the meantime, Portia's suitors are arriving in Belmont to try their luck in a lottery devised by her father. His will directs that each suitor must select one of three caskets, made of gold, silver and lead. He who chooses the casket containing her portrait will win her hand in marriage.

Shylock's daughter Jessica and his servant Launcelot wish to leave the Jew's cheerless house, Jessica to elope with Lorenzo, who is a Gentile, Launcelot to serve Bassanio. Disguised as a boy, Jessica steals money and jewels from her father and escapes with her lover. Shylock, infuriated and held up to the ridicule of the whole Gentile community, recovers his equanimity somewhat on hearing a rumour that Antonio has lost a ship at sea. In course of time it is given out that the merchant has lost *all* his ships and will not be able to pay back the loan within the term allowed. Increasingly obsessed by hate and seizing his opportunity to exact revenge, Shylock has him arrested for debt and gloats over him in prison.

In Belmont two princes, of Morocco and Arragon, enter the lottery, flatter their own self-images, choose gold and silver respectively, find rejections and quickly depart. Bassanio, making a good impression on Portia, after deliberating chooses the lead casket. This turns out to be the right one and he marries Portia, acquiring her money and assets. She gives him a ring as a token of their love and makes him promise never to part with it. Bassanio is no longer poor but his bliss is ended when he hears of Antonio's plight. He goes off to Venice to support his now distraught friend. Portia and her maid Nerissa, who has married Gratiano, disguise themselves as lawyer and lawyer's clerk respectively. They journey to Venice, armed with a letter of introduction from a famous legal kinsman of Portia's in Padua, and leaving Lorenzo and Jessica in charge of the Belmont house.

At the ensuing trial to determine Antonio's contract with Shylock, the Duke of Venice presides. He is partial to Antonio but cannot deny that Shylock has the law on his side. Portia, unrecognised in her judicial robes, arrives to defend Antonio, pleading with Shylock to show mercy to the merchant, but the Jew still insists on the letter of the law and gets ready to cut the flesh nearest to the heart of his enemy.

Shylock is completely confident that both law and lawyer will support him, but just as he is about to use his newly-sharpened knife, Portia warns him that he is entitled only to Antonio's flesh, not to a single drop of his blood. She adds, moreover, that the amount cut must be accurately weighed, or Shylock himself will be liable to severe penalties, even including death. Shylock sees that he must modify his claim, so asks for his money back instead, but Portia then tells him that the law of Venice disallows such a form of restitution and that in arranging for such a bond in the first place he is demonstrably guilty of plotting to kill a Venetian citizen, also a capital offence.

The court rules that the Jew should lose all his assets but Antonio intercedes and asks for a lesser fine to be imposed, on condition that Shylock converts to Christianity and wills his estate to Lorenzo and

Jessica. Shylock, with no choice but to accept, departs defeated, jeered at by Gratiano, who has been keeping up an insulting commentary on the proceedings. By way of legal fee Portia asks for the ring with which her husband had sworn never to part and Nerissa follows suit. Bassanio and Gratiano, not recognising their wives in legal garb, reluctantly hand over their rings.

Back in Belmont, where all the main characters except Shylock now congregate, Lorenzo and Jessica, 'caretaking' for Portia, have been enjoying a worry-free existence and are discovered musing over their happy lot in a wonderful moonlight setting. Portia and Nerissa, now divested of their disguises, return, followed by Bassanio, Gratiano and Antonio. Portia brings good news, informing Antonio that three of his missing ships are safe after all. Lorenzo and Jessica are presented with Shylock's deed of gift, signed and sealed in accordance with the court's decision.

Finally the practical joke involving the rings is revealed to the easy-going husbands, together with the true identities of the lawyer and the clerk. This disconcerts the two men, but all is soon forgiven and the ending for all those in Belmont is apparently a happy one.

3.2 SUMMARIES AND CRITICAL COMMENTARIES

Act I, Scene i

Summary
Antonio, a rich Venetian merchant and ship-owner, is introduced as full of an inexplicable melancholy. His friends Salerio and Solanio think that Antonio is worried about his ships at sea, as they would be in Antonio's position, but the merchant denies that this is the cause of his dejection, as his capital has been distributed widely and not entrusted to any one ship or single financial venture.

Solanio then suggests another reason – love, which Antonio ridicules. Solanio concludes that there is no logical answer. Bassanio, Lorenzo and Gratiano enter and are soon left alone with Antonio. Gratiano observes that Antonio does not look well and is changed. Antonio answers that his role is a sad one, whereupon Gratiano makes a speech, proclaiming unsympathetically that his own is to enjoy life.

After Gratiano and Lorenzo depart, Bassanio comes to the point of his visit (123). He has known Antonio for a long time, has received financial help from him many times before and now wants it again so that he may try to marry Portia, a rich heiress of Belmont. According to him, without funds he will be at a disadvantage compared with the many rich and famous suitors who seek her hand. Antonio is eager to help him but lacks ready cash, so advises Bassanio to use his (Antonio's) name to get credit in Venice.

Commentary
The gloomy opening sets the stage for what at first looks like a tragedy in the making. To conceal the reasons for sadness on the stage was an accepted convention. In a Shakespearean comedy such gloom has generally to do with love, but the audience is never given a clear explanation and is left with forebodings of some future calamity.

The merchant is introduced to the audience as a victim of melancholy, one of the four well-known 'humours', used as another stage convention. The ancient doctrine of humours divided individuals into four distinct personality-types, melancholic, choleric, phlegmatic and sanguine. A humour was thought to be an actual bodily liquid, a physiological element which normally lay in balance with the three others but which in excess threatened to absorb and change the entire personality. Melancholic and choleric (black and red bile respectively) were the most commonly encountered in stage tragedy and the melancholic type was several times exploited by Shakespeare. Jaques in *As You Like It*, Timon in *Timon of Athens* and Hamlet are each dominated by this humour and Antonio's opening words suggest that he has been afflicted by an excess of 'black bile', recognised as a potential source of personal disaster.

References in the first 40 lines to storms and shipwrecks also contribute to this sense of impending doom. The allusion by Solanio to maps for navigational purposes (19) reflects contemporary interest in exploration and suggests the perils faced by voyagers at a time when the Flemish cartographer Gerhardus Mercator's flat map-projection of the world, use of the astrolabe or sextant and the compass were comparatively recent developments.

Antonio's denial that he is concerned about his floating fortunes is less than the truth (as we later discover at line 178, when he reveals himself more frankly to Bassanio alone). It invites the audience to consider that perhaps his gloom does have something to do with the high risk to which his ships have been put. Solanio's joking suggestion that the merchant is in love (46) is what the audience expects but it, too, is pooh-poohed by Antonio. It is implied that personal moods are matters beyond human understanding. In fact, the reason for Antonio's show of melancholia is not itself important in the action, though he seems beset by feelings of insecurity and is not his normal, presumably more cheerful, self.

Gratiano enters with Bassanio and Lorenzo to make a strong contrast between this despondent figure and a light-hearted man like himself. This is the comedy-playwright's way out of the realm of tragedy, for Antonio is exhibiting only the *appearance* of personal affliction. Antonio sees himself as a romantic sufferer but his posture is an unconscious irony, as he is mistaking appearance for reality and deceiving himself that his destined role is tragic when it is not to be. The world does not treat him harshly for long, though at this point the audience does not know what the future holds for this prosperous merchant.

The image of the world as a stage (76–8) was one to which Shakespeare returned, for he used it in *As You Like It, Hamlet, Macbeth*, and notably in *The Tempest*, when Prospero likens 'this insubstantial pageant' (the stage) to his magic island creation and both to the deceptive 'real' world. The idea that everyone is taking part in a human comedy was another dramatic convention, to be summed up by another melancholy character, Jaques. His comment in *As You Like It*, II.vii that 'All the world's a stage, / And all the men and women merely players' has a double significance if taken as an allusion to the Globe theatre.

Bassanio's friend Gratiano is no fool, in spite of his name (in traditional Italian comedy that of a clown, sometimes presented as a doctor). If vocal emphasis in line 79 is put on *me*, it indicates more clearly that this character likes to be the centre of his own stage. Gratiano is another self-styled 'play-actor', himself posing in this scene as a shallow wit and showing a remarkable insensitivity to Antonio's state of mind. Later in the action Gratiano will exhibit even further this lack of sympathy to the plight of others. In this bright speech he attacks puritanism, personified as men of grave aspect (83–5). His images are physiological, related to the origins of human behaviour. The third newcomer, Lorenzo, says very little, leaving us in doubt as to what he is thinking. Each member of this trio will give up his bachelor status before the end of the play.

It is obvious that Bassanio is deeply in debt, and that Antonio, a relative and long-standing friend, is emotionally attached to him. On the surface Antonio's willingness to lend more money without asking questions suggests that he is an open-hearted gentleman, consistently charitable, though his feelings for Bassanio may require a more subtle explanation. Bassanio's excuse for borrowing once again is, he says, a matter of the heart, implying that a poor man will not succeed in love. Reference to a love-match in commercial terms – to which attention is drawn by the word *thrift* (176) – implies profit as well as good fortune (as Shylock points out, I.iii.91). This suggests that love's currency is happiness to which joy is added as interest, compounded to a higher figure. 'Love's wealth' is one of the major themes in the play and is accounted for in detail by John Russell Brown in his introduction to the Arden edition of *The Merchant* and also in his book *Shakespeare and His Comedies* [see 'Further Reading'].

Act I, Scene ii

Summary
In Portia's Belmont palace, the heroine and her waiting-maid and *confidante* Nerissa are talking about the terms of her father's will, which provides that she shall choose a husband by lottery. Nerissa explains the method of this lottery whereby the suitor making the correct choice from gold, silver and lead caskets will win Portia's hand.

The two women discuss the various aristocratic candidates and reject them all derisively. Portia holds a low opinion of her suitors and sneers at every one of them as Nerissa serves up the names in turn, but at the end of this exchange Nerissa reveals that none of these gentlemen is still in the running anyway, a fact apparently unknown to Portia. However, when Nerissa mentions yet another suitor, Portia instantly recalls his name, Bassanio.

We hear that four unsuccessful suitors have already left but that another aspirant, the Prince of Morocco, is on his way. Portia is not enthusiastic, implying that she does not like his colour, and goes off to meet him with a cynical comment.

Commentary
From Venice we move to its contrary, Belmont, a foreign-sounding name suggestive in Italian of an idyllic house built on a hill, the very antithesis of metropolitan commercialism. Portia admits to a less-than-happy state of mind, in her case caused by world-weariness and boredom, a pose typical of the 'poor little rich girl'. This recalls and parallels Antonio's demeanour in the previous scene and Nerissa answers her as Gratiano answered Antonio, after 30 lines turning her attention to a lighter subject.

Portia's talk is fluent and witty, cleverly playing on words in Shakespeare's earlier, flashier style, not employed much in *The Merchant*. From her first long prose statement (13–28), Portia is inclined to use legalistic language (a point worth remembering) and we find out that her discontent partly originates in her father's restrictive legacy. This is not significant in the action nor does it contribute much to an eventual assessment of Portia.

The scene serves to introduce Nerissa, a sharp-tongued, alert personality and a shrewd observer of human nature, not greatly overshadowed by her mistress. Her tone suggests that Nerissa must have noticed at the time that Portia was attracted to Bassanio although this young man's visit had taken place well back in the past when her father was still alive. It was on this former occasion that Bassanio first saw his future in terms of a rich marriage, a conclusion in keeping with contemporary upper-class custom and acceptable to Shakespeare's audiences.

Nerissa's reference to Bassanio as a 'scholar–soldier' places him in an aristocratic class distinguished for accomplishments (including swordsmanship and the composition of light verses) practised in the courts of Italy and France. Contemporary adventurers like Sir Philip Sidney and Sir Walter Raleigh were considered walking examples of this European renaissance ideal, the 'new nobility' so much admired by the Tudors. These men were quite different from the crude, rough-spoken and illiterate mediaeval knight. Ophelia described Hamlet as having been 'the glass of fashion and the mould of form', a model to be followed by other young gallants. Bassanio is a type endowed by Nerissa with similarly admirable qualities, a fit suitor who, if tested, would show that he belonged to a civilised, sophisticated class practising chivalrous conduct and worthy to be Portia's husband. His allusive speech in III.ii and his loyalty to Antonio prove this.

Act I, Scene iii

Summary

Having established what life in Belmont is like, almost though not quite carefree, Shakespeare returns us to Venice, where Bassanio is trying to float a loan for three months on Antonio's credit from Shylock, a Jewish usurer. Shylock has every intention of granting the loan but he goes through the motions of pondering on the business advantages to himself of making it since, although he knows that Antonio is in theory financially sound, the word on the Rialto is that the merchant's assets are largely tied up in risky ventures at sea.

Bassanio invites Shylock to discuss possible arrangements with Antonio over dinner (33), but the Jew roughly rejects the offer on cultural and religious grounds. On Antonio's entry Shylock, pretending not to recognise him and accepting Bassanio's introduction, tells the audience in an 'aside' how he feels towards Antonio and articulates his hate (43), rationalising it on the grounds that Antonio is a Christian who has undercut Shylock's business by lending out money without charging interest. Shylock promises himself a just revenge, rooted in the ancient grudge between Jew and Christian and in what he interprets as Antonio's hatred of Jews.

In the meantime Shylock goes on debating the pros (rather than the cons) of granting the loan and starts working out the interest over twelve months, but before finally agreeing gives vent to his bottled-up bitterness towards Antonio, whose conduct in the past has been offensive to him. He asks rhetorically why he should lend money to someone who has treated him with so much contempt. Antonio not only admits this frankly but is unrepentant. So far as the merchant is concerned this is just a matter of business and the money advanced might with more point be lent to an enemy, for then any penalty incurred could be much more rigorously exacted from the defaulter.

Shylock reveals his terms, as he puts it, 'in a merry sport' (147). He states that if Antonio cannot repay the sum borrowed he must allow a pound of his own flesh to be cut from whatever part of his body the Jew chooses. Antonio accepts, confident that he can redeem the bond a month earlier than the agreement specifies. Antonio himself, anticipating the precepts of Polonius in *Hamlet*, is normally neither lender nor borrower and despises usury. He is only doing this to help Bassanio whose attempt to stop him (155–6) is not very determined. (Later (180) Bassanio's suspicions are in no way allayed after he learns more fully of the arrangement and hears the Jew's talk of forgiveness, a virtue which properly belongs to Christianity and which might be considered alien to Shylock). But the loan is made.

Commentary

The sum needed by Bassanio is about seven hundred pounds, at that time a considerable sum of money and a handsome dowry. The fact that Antonio does not have this amount in ready cash at his disposal suggests that he may be living with no margin. When Shylock equates Antonio's goodness with his 'sufficiency', this is an irony, since Shylock soon shows himself familiar with the details of Antonio's fortune. He knows that it has been set at risk in various parts of the world where anything might happen. Recalling the first scene, we may think that Antonio has good cause to feel sad, since he has spread himself too widely without security.

Yet, in spite of his shaky economic condition, the merchant is ready to hazard his own security for his friend without hesitation. The Elizabethan audience would have recognised this type as a bold merchant–venturer, a high-risk gambler and swashbuckler like the Queen's favourite Sir Walter Raleigh. But Antonio does not strike us as a confident plunger in the venturer mould. The impression he makes is rather that of a man to be respected because he puts friendship before financial considerations, something which Shylock cannot understand. Shakespeare may have thought that there was not much difference between the taking of risk at sea for the chance of high profits as the admired merchant–venturers did and the practice of usury for which the Jews were so much despised.

Shylock's impolite rejection of Bassanio's offer to dine makes his religious and cultural objections clear and shows how far apart he stands from the Christian characters in the play. By his avowed determination to take on the role of 'revenger' for his tribe (and really for himself), Shylock presents himself to Shakespeare's audience in a familiar theatrical role, that of a man fired by hate and vowing vengeance. The parable recalling Jacob and Laban (73ff) taxes Antonio's patience and explains what Jews consider the true nature of interest to be. It is derived from a Genesis story about Jacob who kept for himself the new-born lambs from a flock he cared for on behalf of his uncle Laban. Shylock is proud of Jacob's business sense (90) and incidentally of his own talents in that direction. His contention (97) relates money which fails to 'breed' to a barren animal. Somewhere about this stage in the action Shylock conceives the germ of his plot, and the rest of this scene (145f) explains the conditions attaching to the loan.

The Jacob–Laban story is Shylock's defence of usury, but not a successful one. His point seems to be that in business sentiment has no place. Antonio, irritated and anxious to get a decision, rejects the parallel. His animated reply (98–103) is the only occasion in the play where the merchant sheds his cloak of melancholy and shows a spark of life. His images ('devil', 'evil soul', 'villain', 'rotten apple' and 'falsehood') imply that Shylock is a wicked and corrupt deceiver. Antonio is seen to throw caution to the winds, challenge fate and practically invite Shylock to do his worst.

The irony here is that Antonio still goes on with the arrangement, buoyed up with optimism as false as the 'goodly apple' (a contrast with the 'rotten' one) of his metaphor. As the action continues it becomes clearer to the audience that Antonio is walking into some kind of trap. His refusal to perceive what to the audience is obvious puts him in the category of a rigid figure, marching towards his own doom and therefore potentially comic as well as tragic.

The passage (107ff) has one strong image – that of the persecuted Jew, suffering with resignation. But whereas dramatic suffering usually increases stature, as in Greek drama and in the great tragedies, *King Lear* in particular, this account diminishes Shylock. It is a revelation of insults received by Shylock and symbolically by all Jews in connection with their money-lending. Antonio's reported behaviour is ugly and he brazens it out, a reaction which also reduces him. We begin to see his shortcomings.

'I would be friends with you', Shylock tells Antonio (139) in return for the latter's rejection of a species of friendship which involves the payment of interest. So far Antonio has been friendly enough and is ready to be amiable but, as we shall discover, this is a mask hiding the reality of his dislike which amounts to contempt for Shylock and all he represents. Note that Shylock's demeanour changes abruptly when he offers Antonio friendship and it is clear that he too is camouflaging his real feelings. Their exchanges in this scene shed light on Shylock's priorities, which are entirely self-interested, whereas Antonio's are not.

Shylock equates his terms for lending with 'kindness', which has two senses – generous and according to nature – implying goodness and fellow-feeling. What Bassanio means by 'This were kindness' (144) becomes clearer if followed by a question-mark, indicating doubt. Some editors, following the eighteenth-century poet Alexander Pope's suggestion, gave this line to Antonio, thinking that it led toward the merchant's acceptance at line 153 but it makes more sense if Bassanio, who wants the loan, says these words, even if disapprovingly.

The human flesh forfeit is presented as a substitute for cash interest (showing that Shylock is not just after money but something perhaps more sinister) and Antonio agrees immediately. It might be thought that Shylock shows himself to be unwise in not realising that (as Portia later reveals) such an arrangement is illegal. There is irony here, but its full effect is to be delayed until Act IV. The well-known surgical penalty is not original to Shakespeare and occurs in *Il Pecorone*, (translatable into English as 'The Dunce' or 'Simpleton') a fourteenth-century Italian tale by Giovanni Fiorentino and the main source of Shakespeare's plot.

By this time we are beginning to understand something of the connection and contrast between Venice and Belmont. The link is Bassanio's fortune-hunting, which will eventually cause the main characters to come together, since money as a means of solving life's problems is one of the main issues in the play. Money is both the agent of Bassanio's success in love and of Shylock's advantage over Antonio, yet here we have Shylock refusing money in favour of an item which he himself admits has no intrinsic value, a pound of human flesh. 'Pound' suggests to an English audience a measurement both of weight and currency.

Bassanio's last remark is a warning to Antonio (unnecessary so far as the audience is concerned) that Antonio's confidence in Shylock's goodwill is misplaced. We see the situation here through the eyes of Bassanio who, in spite of his distrust of the Jew, puts his own interests first and does not try very hard to stop Antonio from putting himself at hazard in this strange fashion.

Shylock, shown to be positively anti-Christian just as Antonio is negatively anti-Jewish, emerges as a hater and revenger, cunning and devious, confirming the audience's representative view of Jews. For example, he hints that he is short of ready money and will have to borrow the three thousand from another rich Jew, Tubal, but later we learn that Shylock kept cash in his house, since his daughter steals it in II.vi. We are made uneasy by his unusual bond, however lightly contemplated, for Antonio's confidence and the ludicrous nature of the penalty for default, together with Shylock's airy talk about it, encourage our suspicions that Antonio's future may not be as bright as he thinks. Seeing the play for the first time, we cannot put ourselves in Antonio's place, since he is obviously making a mistake which we think we ourselves would not have made. We thus feel superior to him. This sense of personal elevation lies at the very root of comedy.

Act II, Scene i

Summary
In Belmont the lottery is still open, with the Prince of Morocco ready to try for Portia's hand. He and his train enter to the sound of trumpets and he has a short dignified exchange with Portia, agreeing never to marry should his choice of casket prove wrong.

Commentary
The effect of this short scene of 50 lines, opening with a blast of cornets, is mainly ceremonial, a contrast to the drabness of I.iii. If Morocco is dressed in white robes, his dark skin colour (which we already know Portia does not like) will be set off. Morocco is aware of its effects on others, and Portia's reply, which hints at the unattractive list of previous competitors and includes a pun on 'fair' (20) rules him out in her estimation and makes her reject him on a personal basis, though he does not see this. Portia's assurances are no more than appropriately polite under the circumstances and not as flattering as they sound.

Morocco, one of three 'outsiders' in the play, is an impressive nobleman full of pride, who not only makes it clear that he believes marriage to him would be a privilege for any maiden but also declares that he would even change his colour to attract Portia's attention, an absurdity. His talk is all of himself and his military prowess, but after his high-flown bragging declamation he suddenly realises (31) that such boasting will not assist him to a correct choice of casket. The two speakers each harp on the idea of chance (*choice*, *lottery*, *destiny*, *choosing*, *fortune*, *dice*, *hazard*) planting the idea of luck in the draw of marriage in the mind of the audience who now await Morocco's actual draw in a future scene.

Act II, Scene ii

Summary
After Morocco's pompous showing, we return to Venice for a scene of part-comic relief. Gobbo, Shylock's servant, is debating with himself whether or not he ought to remain in the Jew's employ. He makes comparison between two fiends, the Devil himself who tells him to leave and the Jew, whom he calls 'the very devil incarnation'. Of the two he prefers the advice of the first, which is to run away.

Old Gobbo, Launcelot's father and almost blind, enters and a comic exchange follows, based initially on the old man's failure to recognise his own son, and full of confusion deriving from misuse of language and Launcelot's deliberate attempt to mislead him. Launcelot finally makes up his mind to leave Shylock, prompted by the sight of Bassanio, whom he thinks would be a better master. Bassanio tells him that Shylock has agreed to his departure and accepts him, ordering a new livery to denote Launcelot's improved status.

Gratiano enters, seeking to go to Belmont with Bassanio and gets permission immediately, but Bassanio advises him to modify his conduct which might damage Bassanio's chances of success. Gratiano solemnly promises to adapt himself to these fresh surroundings, but only after he has enjoyed a final night of pleasure in Venice.

Commentary
This is a 'visual' episode which lays the burden on each performer in turn and does not come off unless it is energetically 'acted', with facial gestures and much bodily movement. Launcelot confuses meanings and invents new expressions in the experimental style of the Tudors (for example, 'incarnation', and 'gravel-blind') and his imaginary discussion between the fiend and his own conscience is a take-off of the mediaeval morality play in which virtues and vices were personified. Old Gobbo is a character descended from the personified Vice of the old admonitory drama and a rustic type still popular with modern audiences, even if his talk is partly incomprehensible. Shakespeare, masking his subject in cross-talk and clownish blundering, is subtly calling attention to the theme of deception, later manifested in the disguises of Portia, Nerissa and Jessica.

The wordy prose also serves to shed further light on Shylock and is based on popular contemporary notions of what Gentiles think of Jews. Launcelot's comparison of the Jew to the Devil is one of many in the play. 'Jew' is used a dozen times during the exchange between himself and Old Gobbo, either descriptively or pejoratively, leaving a powerful image of Shylock, 'a very Jew' (that is, typical of his race) as a mean employer. Launcelot's concluding comment on himself: 'I am a Jew if I serve the Jew any longer' (122) is evidence that this noun was then a synonym for narrowness, meanness or heartlessness.

The last part of the action predicts a coming change in Gratiano's outward behaviour and draws attention to a further distinction separating Venice from Belmont, where a more elegant style of social conduct is expected. In Venice, however, Gratiano remains his boisterous self – 'too wild, too rude, and bold of voice' to be acceptable in such an environment where it may place Bassanio's suit at risk. In this scene our attention has been directed to the importance of good social manners and of making a favourable impression, a mild form of deception. We know that Gratiano can play other roles just as competently and 'use all the observance of civility' (good manners) if he wishes. Of all the Gentile characters he alone will show (IV, i) a real mastery of invective, the crudest shade in the satiric spectrum.

Act II, Scene iii

Summary
In this short scene of 21 lines Jessica has learned that Launcelot is leaving her father. She gives him a tip to show her appreciation of his past services and to get him to act on her behalf by secretly delivering a letter to Lorenzo. Her brief soliloquy informs us that she is estranged from Shylock and that she hopes to marry Lorenzo and become a Christian.

Commentary
For the first time we learn of the Lorenzo–Jessica romantic love-relationship. These revelations of Jessica's domestic life add to our image of Shylock's as harsh and joyless. 'Our house is hell' she tells Launcelot, whose amusing personality has been her only relief from its drabness. Launcelot calls her 'sweet Jew', thus establishing her separation from her father. Her intimation when alone that she will be converted to Christianity on marriage to Lorenzo further distances her from Shylock, whose isolation from the audience is growing. So far we have not been able to summon up much sympathy for him and can easily understand why his own daughter, though still aware of her filial obligations, is alienated from him. The audience can hardly be surprised that this man, who professes hatred, is himself widely despised.

Shylock is gradually taking on an oppressive shape as an unfeeling monster, lacking in the capacity to judge himself, hostile to life's pleasures and fixed on his own narrow concerns with money and property, a man loveless and unloved.

Act II, Scene iv

Summary
In Venice Gratiano, Lorenzo and Antonio's friends Salerio and Solanio, are getting ready to go to a masque when Launcelot brings in Jessica's letter. Gratiano is curious to know its contents and, alone with Lorenzo, hears from him Jessica's plans for their elopement, and learns about her dowry and her male disguise. In the meantime Launcelot has one other message to deliver. Bassanio has invited Shylock to dine with him.

Commentary
The motif of disguise on which the main plot turns is hinted at, though the audience may be disappointed that the masque is not actually staged in this play as in other Shakespearean plays, such as *A Midsummer Night's Dream* and *The Tempest*. The word 'disguise' (2) refers to the fantastic garb of the masquers, which concealed their

identities and gave them licence to behave as they would not normally do in public.

Jessica, a woman of action with a practical mind, like the other women in the play, is about to adopt disguise to attain her personal ends. Lorenzo unhesitatingly reveals the details of the plot to Gratiano, which may be thought the sign of a loose tongue, but this is done for the benefit of the audience and to speed up the action. It diminishes Shylock still farther and excuses Jessica's conduct on the grounds that she has a non-Christian for a father – 'faithless' implies denial of Christianity, then a serious offence for which one could be imprisoned.

The main dramatic effect of this scene is to stress urgency and build up a sense of anticipation in the audience. Things are happening quickly and we learn about meetings, appointments, arrangements and conspiracy, one after the other.

Act II, Scene v

Summary
We now listen to a conversation before Shylock's house. Shylock receives Bassanio's invitation through Launcelot, agrees to accept 'in hate', the meanest of reasons, and learns that the invitation will include a masque, which he dislikes. Jessica is instructed to look after the house in his absence and Launcelot manages to tell Jessica out of Shylock's hearing that 'a Christian' will be passing. She understands that he means Lorenzo. Shylock shows his contempt for Bassanio, in his view a lazy, greedy fellow. The scene ends on the words of Jessica, now completely alienated from her father and relying on her plan to change her own life.

Commentary
Here we find Shylock at home, no attractive personality, with a sour outlook on life. He has a deep-rooted antipathy to entertainments like the masque and to its piping which he calls 'vile squealing'. The adjective 'wry-neck'd' refers to the unavoidable contortions of the player's features and body. Rivalry between the lyre of Apollo and the pipe of Pan was of ancient origin and one of the Roman poet Horace's *Odes* counsels avoidance of 'the lowly pipes'.

Shylock's aversion springs not from his knowledge of the classics but from his hatred of those Christians who take part in such celebrations wearing disguises or make-up. Up to this point our sympathies are entirely with Jessica, whose final couplets emphasise her alienation from this hard parent and enlist our support of her plan to escape from his dreary supervision.

Act II, Scene vi

Summary
Dressed as masquers, Gratiano and Salerio are waiting for Lorenzo outside Shylock's house. Lorenzo is late in turning up and Gratiano reveals something of his shallow philosophy in lines 12–13. Lorenzo has hardly appeared when Jessica, disguised as a boy, calls down from the balcony above and having identified Lorenzo in the poor light throws down a casket of valuables saying that she will get more ducats and join him, which she does immediately.

They all go off to the masque except for Gratiano, who learns from Antonio that the ship is about to sail for Belmont with Bassanio waiting for him on board.

Commentary
This is a time-marking interlude, to give the boy playing Jessica a chance to change clothing. Its full effect may only be realised in actual performance, since we meet only two masquers and hear the sounds of revelry from a distance. When Jessica, in her own disguise, throws down the casket and promises to get 'more ducats' (49) it is brought home to the audience that perhaps their sympathy for her in the previous scene has to be modified since, after all, what she is doing is stealing. Gratiano's praise of her actions and Lorenzo's praise of her as 'wise, fair, and true' (56) have thus to be taken ironically, since Jessica has certainly not been 'true' to her father.

Antonio's appearance reminds us of Bassanio's business in Belmont, of the bond and of another kind of chance-taking, the hazard of a sea-voyage, though the wind is favourable and the atmosphere, as Gratiano's concluding word suggest, is one of optimism. Note that the revellers never get to the masque (64).

Act II, Scene vii

Summary
This continues the action in Belmont from II.i. Morocco makes his choice of casket, reading out the three inscriptions and analysing his own reactions to each one in turn. Portia utters an encouraging comment, assuring him that the correct choice of the one containing her portrait will make her his wife.

Eventually he decides on the gold casket, after making an unsubtle connection of gold with 'what many men desire', that is, with Portia. The content of the casket turns out to be a skull with a scroll pointing out that this suitor has been lured into error by outward show. Seeing that he has lost, Morocco goes at once. Portia is glad to see him off, making a final comment on his colour.

Commentary

The setting is ceremonial, with a trumpet fanfare as opening, and the movements of Morocco and his train stately and deliberate, a contrast to the previous scene of rapid action. Portia's comment after her suitor has read out the inscriptions hints at the strange combination of gambling and choice of marriage-partner which governs the situation.

Morocco, entrusting judgement to fate, has an unsubtle mind and interprets the inscriptions literally, at the same time piling extravagant flattery upon the lady in quasi-religious language, (39ff) the stock lovers' flattery popular with young Elizabethan gallants which Shakespeare, and more especially the poet John Donne, liked to ridicule. Gold and silver have more appeal for him than base lead and he picks the gold casket, associating Portia with 'an angel' (a pun on the name given to a contemporary coin). Imagery here is predictably associated with the three metals conventionally denoting (gold) royalty or riches, (silver) chill purity and (lead) equity.

The content, a skull reproduced in the style of contemporary emblem books, accompanied by a scroll offering advice, is in the late mediaeval tradition of *memento mori*, which reduced earthly values to nothing with effigies of death. Such an object was intended to bring the beholder to a sense of his own impotence and inevitable fate and the persistence of such imagery throughout the Reformation in art and poetry testifies to a deep-rooted pessimism which affected the Elizabethans more than is generally recognised. Though we hear much about Tudor 'zest for life' and their joy in it as a great gift, this was less often expressed in the later years of the century, when writers tended either to exaggerate the place of man on the hierarchical 'scale of being', and place him on a level not far below that of the divine or to contemplate the possibility of life's futility, reflecting the uncertainty which accompanied a relatively rapid shift away from the securer beliefs of the Middle Ages. Shakespeare later used the device to great effect in the grave-digging scene when Hamlet picked up Yorick's skull and mused on man's mortality.

The emblem book was very popular in Italy and France and was widely reproduced elsewhere. The best-known English one was Geoffrey Whitney's *Emblems* (1586) known to Shakespeare and Spenser. An 'emblem' (*impresa*) is a printed picture or image combined with a symbolic motto explaining its meaning, often rather tediously. Elizabethan dramatists took many devices from these books and the skull image was common. Interpretation of these visual symbols is called iconography.

Though the skull may seem inappropriate as a response to the casket's inscription ('Who chooseth me shall gain what many men desire'), whereas the writing on the scroll refers directly to the misleading character of a gilded exterior ('All that glisters is not gold'), the implication is that Morocco, by choosing the wrong casket, has been shown more than one image of life's hollowness and deceit, since the inscription itself is misleading. Gold is equated with death in Chaucer's *Pardoner's Tale*.

Morocco's abrupt departure may suggest his shallow character and the triviality of his protestations of love since it is clear that his only love is himself, the man with a 'golden mind' as he says. Portia's relief, stated in 'a gentle riddance' at least shows that she respects Morocco for having taken his defeat with dignity. Her final comment on his colour would not have produced the effect on a contemporary audience which it would nowadays.

Act II, Scene viii

Summary
We are transported over the sea to Venice, where we learn of the hue and cry that follows hard upon Shylock's discovery of Jessica's elopement. Antonio had assured the Duke of Venice that the lovers were not on board ship with Bassanio though it appears that they circulated a false rumour to divert pursuers. Solanio, who with Salerio acts as a reporter for the audience's benefit, mocks Shylock's wrath at Jessica's disobedience, her flight with a Christian and her theft of her father's ducats and valuables. Solanio passes on another rumour to add to the disquiet. A Venetian ship has been lost in the Channel and it may be Antonio's. Solanio comments on Antonio's charitable disposition and particularly on his affection for Bassanio (50).

Commentary
Solanio's making of Shylock an object of public ridicule is balanced by the Jew's predisposition to revenge, noted in lines 25–6. The scene shows a change for the worse in Shylock. He has been personally hurt by his daughter's treachery, by her association with a Christian and the loss of his money and jewels. He has been publicly humiliated and derided by street urchins. Salerio's comment on this prepares us for Shylock's reaction if Antonio, as now appears likely, is prevented from 'keeping his day'.

This scene provides the first definite indication that Antonio may default on his loan. Though he does not know it, the means and opportunity to extract the vengeance he yearns for seem to be about to fall into Shylock's hand and direct his motives to a specific end. Salerio and Solanio are the agents of reported action by which the audience may imagine Shylock's present discomfiture and the despondent mood of Antonio.

Act II, Scene ix

Summary
The lottery action is continued from II.vii, this time with the Prince of Arragon in the suitor's role. Like Morocco he muses on the three inscriptions, eventually choosing the silver casket which contains the portrait of a fool's head and a motto comparing him to fools who like the casket are 'silvered o'er', that is, dressed up to look worthier than they are. Confronted by his failure, Arragon tries to save some dignity through cynicism. He retires, leaving Portia and Nerissa to comment on fate's decisions. Portia is glad to see the last of Arragon.

As Nerissa draws the curtain concealing the caskets a messenger arrives bringing news of the imminent arrival of another suitor, preceded by valuable gifts carried by 'a young Venetian' whose appearance has greatly impressed the messenger. (This is presumably Gratiano.) Nerissa has the last word and hopes that the new suitor will be Bassanio.

Commentary
Arragon's processional is similar to Morocco's in II.i and II.vii. The conditions of the lottery are re-confirmed to remind the audience of the penalty of wrong choice. Arragon, as his name suggests, holds a very high opinion of himself and, although he appears to be less outwardly pompous than Morocco, he is no more worthy, showing that he is full of contempt for his fellows. He should have an equally magnificent train to help emphasise his loss of dignity.

Note that Arragon is speechless when he first opens the casket, then that he reads the verse and continues it in the same rhythm, laughing at himself, a gesture which redeems him somewhat in the eyes of the audience. His argument is one of sham logic and omits the love factor entirely. Like Morocco, Arragon judges by the very standard he affects to despise, outward show, and the result of his choice, 'the portrait of a blinking idiot', is his fall from high dignity to absurdity in an instant. The French philosopher Henri Bergson claimed that such a sudden plunge contained the essence of the comic.

The image of the fool or jester, conventionally symbolising a sectarian heretic or scoffer at religious mysteries, was taken, like that of the skull, from the emblem books and becomes with its motto a comment on 'shadow and substance' (another way of referring to appearance and reality). Portia's comment at line 60–1 after Arragon has protested anticipates the legalistic moralising of the trial to come.

Scene ix is the last of a series of panoramic sweeps between Venice, where Shylock's revenge is being fed by his daughter's treachery and the loss of his assets, and Belmont, where material considerations and self-love dictate wrong choices. These sweeps also serve to mark the passage of time, which is running out for Antonio.

The audience now knows two things: that the winning casket must be the leaden one and that Bassanio is the favourite runner in the marriage stakes. The scene ends on a note of pleasant expectancy.

Act III, Scene i

Summary
Antonio's friends Solanio and Salerio continue (from II.viii) the spread of the disquieting rumours of the merchant's losses. Shylock approaches and is shown no sympathy when he complains about his daughter's conduct and with little encouragement makes it clear that he intends to collect his bond, justifying his proposed action by reiterating Antonio's personal offences as explained in I.iii. He asks a series of rhetorical questions, asserting that Christians and Jews share a common humanity and consequently a common tendency and entitlement to seek revenge.

A messenger enters saying that Antonio is looking for Solanio and Salerio and they depart, giving place to Tubal, another Jew and Shylock's only apparent friend in the play. Tubal stirs him up with more unwelcome information about his daughter's flight. She has been traced to Genoa but not found. Shylock complains bitterly to Tubal about his growing losses but brightens when Tubal strengthens further the rumour about Antonio's missing ship.

The rumour now becomes a reported fact. Tubal returns to the bad news that Jessica has been squandering money in Genoa and, worse, that she has sold her mother's ring in return for 'a monkey' (possibly a slang term for a fixed sum of money, nowadays five hundred pounds, rather than an animal). When Antonio's loss is again mentioned, Shylock resolves to proceed to his revenge in full and asks Tubal to set in motion the legal machinery for arresting the merchant.

Commentary
This scene is entirely in prose, underlining the harshness of the content. The love of Belmont prepares to combat the hate emanating from Venice. From optimism in the former we turn to Shylock's relentless obsession, though at first Shylock is calmer than Solanio's report in II.viii made him out to be. Solanio and Salerio herald his approach by calling him 'the devil . . . in the likeness of a Jew' (21–3) and proceed to goad him. The flesh Shylock intends to claim is for him only a token symbol of his revenge, of no intrinsic worth but a tangible return for past insults inspired as he thinks by one motive only, namely, that he is a Jew.

His hatred of Christians in general and of Antonio in particular has intensified since Shylock's last appearance at II.v. It is obvious that Shylock, well furnished with motives in Act I, will be absolutely ruthless now that he has a chance to strike at his enemies. His string of impassioned rhetorical questions (61ff) claims a common humanity for Christians and Jews and consequently a like tendency to desire and to take revenge, though the violence of his intended reaction far exceeds the alleged offences against him personally. However, it is clear that this species of revenge on this particular Christian, however extreme, is in his own mind justified and he even credits Christians in general with teaching him how to extract it. It is at this point that Shylock reaches a low point in the audience's estimation, ironically at the end of his apparently logical claim to a physical sensitivity equal to that of a Christian.

Tubal, similarly condemned by Solanio, is there to convey information but his account of Jessica's actions seems excessively detailed, and unkind to Shylock. Shylock's daughter has cut herself off from the family completely, even from her dead mother's memory, represented by the ring. Tubal's 'friendship' with Shylock is based on a business relationship and one ought to remember Shylock's own reference to him at I.iii.58. Note here (112ff) what eighteenth-century critics called a 'transition', that is, the near-simultaneous expression by Shylock of more than one emotional reaction, in this instance the effect of the loss of his daughter and his ducats touched by a memory of his dead wife Leah, which in the next moment is submerged in hatred for Antonio.

Act III, Scene ii

Summary
In strong contrast, Bassanio is found at Belmont preparing to try his luck with the caskets. Portia says that she is not in love but would like him to stay in Belmont for a month before choosing and that if she could tell him which casket to choose without breaking her promise to her father she would do so. Bassanio professes his love in a less selfish manner than either Morocco or Arragon and Portia tells him to make his choice, which true love will ensure is the right one. Before he does so a song, commanded by Portia, is heard.

Bassanio makes a speech leading to his choice of the leaden casket. In an aside Portia tells the audience that he has chosen correctly. He finds Portia's portrait and a motto to the effect that he who has not chosen by appearances has won. He pays the portrait extravagant compliments, is welcomed by Portia and assured of his new status. Portia makes a very modest statement of her own virtues and accomplishments (158–62) and gives him a ring as a token of her relinquishment of ownership, a token which he is instructed to keep always as a guarantee of his love. He eagerly promises on pain of death never to let it out of his hands. Gratiano in the meantime has extracted a promise of marriage from Nerissa, conditional on the success of Bassanio's suit.

In the midst of this celebration, Lorenzo, Jessica and Salerio enter. Salerio has brought Bassanio a letter from Antonio, containing bad news, which Bassanio immediately shares with Portia and the others. He tells her the truth about his own financial standing and how his own affluent appearance concealed the reality of debt, which has placed his friend in the hands of an enemy. We learn that the letter states that all Antonio's ships have been lost and that even if Antonio could find the money needed to repay the bond. Shylock, according to Salerio, would still refuse it, disregarding pleas by the Duke of Venice himself. Jessica recalls previous threats by her father that he would rather have the flesh than twenty times the money.

When Portia learns that the sum involved is three thousand ducats she indicates that, by her standards, this is a negligible sum and she tells Bassanio to go to Venice and pay it off, twentyfold if need be. Taking control of the situation, she orders the marriage ceremony. At her request Bassanio reads out Antonio's letter asking him to come to Venice 'at my death', since there is no other way in which he can pay Shylock.

Commentary
We have reached the crisis of the play. The third casket scene is tensely awaited, though the audience now realises that it will have a favourable outcome for Bassanio. It follows hard upon the revelation of Antonio's approaching disaster. Portia's claim that her feeling for him is not love is self-deception in view of her other favourable remarks. However, she is in Fortune's hands and will not reveal which casket is the lucky one, for herself as well as for Bassanio. Note that the absurd condition of not remarrying is mentioned both to Morocco and to the second suitor, Arragon, but not to Bassanio. Portia's observations on the power of music at marriage celebrations make the audience aware of its relevance to the action. Her words, 'Now he goes' (53) refer to Bassanio's movement towards the caskets and Portia now thinks of herself extravagantly as a sacrifice, helpless and dependent on her heroic rescuer. The song she commands:

> Tell me where is Fancy bred –
> Or in the heart, or in the head? (line 63)

is important. It is what musicologists call an 'adult' song, with a glimpse of the dark world where fancy dies. *Much Ado About Nothing, As You Like It* and *Twelfth Night* contain similar philosophical insertions. It amounts to a warning against the short-lived power of visual allurement and Bassanio's speech (73ff) is based on this familiar theme. Portia is governed by reason much more than is Bassanio, whose selection is urged by cynicism and pessimism.

The lines 97–101 sum up the now familiar theme of appearance as distinguished from reality and look forward to IV.i when the deceptive character of the law is revealed. Bassanio and Portia are to some degree deceiving each other and she herself. Her modesty is exaggerated since she is no 'unlessoned girl, unschooled, unpractised' (160), as we shall soon discover, while his professions of love are related to material considerations. Nevertheless it is made clear that she is becoming increasingly attracted by Bassanio.

Lorenzo and Jessica's elopement is disorderly, particularly when compared with the Bassanio–Portia marriage. Though the runaways are well received at Belmont Jessica's readiness to report on her father's intentions (285–91) reminds the audience that some sympathy is due to Shylock. Note how Portia sums up the situation when she sees Bassanio's reaction to Antonio's letter, though she does not actively take control until she has heard what the others have to say. Her decisions are clear-cut and unhesitatingly given, a quality which has been apparent in her from her first entrance at I.ii.

Apart from the trial scene, this is the longest scene in the play. In it the result of the lottery is decided, the baleful intentions of Shylock are becoming obvious, the practical, 'managing' personality of Portia is emerging as she starts to act in the interests of Bassanio's friend Antonio and Bassanio himself is revealing that he has a capacity for loyalty. In particular, it enables Belmont and Venice to be linked together through Portia. These elements each assume a more definite shape as the action moves inexorably towards what seems to be a fatal *dénouement*.

Act III, Scene iii

Summary
In Venice Shylock crows with delight at seeing his enemy so reduced and will not listen to Antonio's pleas, insisting that he wants 'my bond' and nothing else. On his departure, Solanio calls him 'an impenetrable cur' and predicts that the Duke will never allow the bond, but Antonio, saying that he has incurred the Jew's hate for paying the debts of others who owed Shylock money, knows that the Duke cannot bring the law into discredit by making an exception. He hopes only that Bassanio will witness the final act.

Commentary
This gloomy scene, with gaoler in attendance, sharpens the audience's impression of Antonio's predicament. Shylock is triumphant, Antonio helpless, unable to see any prospect of escaping the Jew's merciless aims, supported as they are, or so he believes, by the law of Venice. His explanation of Shylock's implacable hostility is oversimple but the audience has heard a full catalogue of Shylock's

reasons and one can only marvel at the merchant's *naïveté*. Yet Antonio, a realist now that he is confronted by the hard fact of his approaching death, regards the situation with equanimity, though he is isolated except for Bassanio (from whom he expects only the support of the latter's physical presence when the debt is paid).

The strongest element in this scene and indeed in the entire act so far is to be found in the spirit of friendship on which Antonio now relies in his surrender to the inevitable.

Act III, Scene iv

Summary

Lorenzo opens the scene by complimenting Portia on her 'god-like amity' in bearing Bassanio's absence for the sake of his friend. Portia classes Antonio with Bassanio on the grounds of their friendship and is resolved to help him (and herself) out of love for Bassanio. She makes her plan. First, she asks Lorenzo and Jessica to act as caretakers at Belmont while she, Portia, enters a nearby monastery to await Bassanio's return from Venice. We will soon learn that this is a ruse and that Portia is really going to Venice herself in disguise, provided with a letter of reference obtained from a Paduan lawyer of standing, Bellario. She sends a servant, Balthazar, to get these, revealing to Nerissa that she intends to pose as a young man in order to complete a plan which she does not describe. She asks Nerissa to dress as a male and instructs her how to behave as a member of the opposite sex.

Commentary

The serious side of Portia's character is now showing itself more and more plainly. Lorenzo's opening remarks lead into a continuation of the last lines of the previous scene, which spoke of Antonio's trust in his friend Bassanio's loyalty. Portia has already heard of Antonio's friendship with her husband-to-be. This is also a 'bond', but not the kind of bond owed to Shylock. Her genuine affection for Bassanio, which up till now might have been thought of as having sprung mainly from the lottery bargain, is underlined by her confession at lines 18–21.

Her plan for 'redeeming' Antonio is revealed gradually. It depends on disguise, as did Jessica's scheme for escape from her father's house. Portia's outline of what she thinks is the typical behaviour of a fashionable courtly lover (63ff) has less force today than on the Elizabethan stage when women's parts were always played by adolescent boys. In this instance the audience is being presented with a boy actor acting the part of a woman acting the part of a boy, a situation which carries its own peculiar attractions.

Act III, Scene v

Summary
Launcelot and Jessica exchange social comment. This is topical, reflecting contemporary humour, some of it crude. Later Lorenzo joins them and asks what she thinks of Bassanio's wife. Jessica extols Bassanio's heavenly fortune in winning Portia's hand.

Commentary
The first half of this light interlude is comic relief and the whole imparts a sense of the passage of time. It could be cut without much effect on the action. Jessica is now a Christian and indulges in unkind witticisms, some of them at the expense of Jewish dietary habits (25–8, 33–7). Lorenzo's contribution is in a similar vein. He teases her about the sins of the fathers, drawing on Exodus and the Second Commandment. The relation of their talk to the main plot is only apparent when Jessica pays Portia elaborate compliments and extols Bassanio's heavenly fortune in winning her hand. It is clear that in her view Portia is the better of the two, also that Jessica has her reservations about Bassanio. A parallel between Bassanio–Portia and Lorenzo–Jessica is hinted at, but their dialogue does little more than establish Jessica as the shrewder partner and Lorenzo as rather weak and ineffectual.

Act IV, Scene i

Summary
This is the famous trial scene, set in a Venetian court presided over by the Duke with other important personages and with the principals on the defending side present. The Duke, whose attempts to change Shylock's mind have evidently failed, expresses sympathy for Antonio, whereupon Antonio shows his determination to endure stoically, accepting the inevitable judgement against him.

Shylock is called. The Duke starts the proceedings by appealing once more to his humanity, with no success. Shylock breaks into one of his obsessional diatribes. giving no reason for his behaviour other than 'a lodg'd hate and a certain loathing' (60) for Antonio. Bassanio is appalled at this response and tries to take up the argument, but Shylock ignores him even when he offers twice the amount of the bond. The Duke repeats his plea for mercy, this time indirectly (88) but Shylock affects not to understand him. He wants only the legal judgement and, if the law is cruel, he claims that it is equally cruel when used to the advantage of Christians, in upholding slavery, for example. He concludes by demanding immediate judgement.

The Duke has only one recourse, to let the learned Balthazar, a lawyer from Padua, take up the defence. Bassanio offers his own flesh, but Antonio condemns himself and prepares to accept his fate. Nerissa enters, disguised as a lawyer's clerk, and Shylock produces a knife which he begins to sharpen in anticipation. He is quite impervious to intermittent verbal volleys from Gratiano and replies only that he stands for 'law'.

The Duke reads out a highly complimentary testimonial from the respected Bellario in support of Portia (called 'Balthazar' in the letter and not to be confused with one of Portia's servants of a similar name), after which Portia herself appears, attired as a Doctor of Laws. We have never associated her with formal legal qualifications but presumably Bellario's letter is to be taken as genuine, as her credit is established to the court's satisfaction. Portia starts to question the appellants. Antonio freely admits liability, whereupon Portia launches into her 'mercy' speech, recalling Christ's Sermon on the Mount. Shylock is still unmoved and answers simply 'I crave the law' (205). Portia soon reverts to strictly legal tactics.

Bassanio once again offers to pay Shylock off, tenfold this time, but Portia informs him that such a course is not legal. She tries herself to get Shylock to agree to a money settlement but he declines. He is now certain that the law is completely on his side and moreover that Portia is interpreting it in his favour. He calls her 'a Daniel come to judgement' (222), referring to a clever lawyer of ancient tradition.

Portia than declares the bond forfeit and makes one final attempt to get Shylock to show mercy, but the Jew will have nothing but his pound of flesh and abruptly rejects a further offer of money. Portia appears to go along with this strictly legal decision and Antonio makes ready to pay the forfeit by baring his breast to the accompaniment of Shylock's gloatings and the production of scales to weigh the flesh.

Shylock refuses Antonio a surgeon to stop the wounds because 'tis not in the bond' (261). He gets ready to cut and Antonio to die. The latter takes his farewell of Bassanio, who replies that he places Antonio's life higher in his estimation than 'life itself, my wife and all the world' (283). Gratiano expresses a similar sentiment. Portia and Nerissa hear and comment on this. Shylock in an aside refers to his daughter's marriage to a Christian.

Portia then draws attention to the exact wording of the bond, which refers to 'a pound of flesh' but not to any 'jot of blood'. Gratiano acts as her chorus five times during the exchange following, which shows Shylock that a literal interpretation of the law can have two sides. He first switches his direction and climbs down further and further from his original lofty position, saying finally that he will take back his own principal, the original three thousand ducats, and call it quits. Bassanio has it ready for him but Portia stops this action, reminding the court that Shylock has already refused such an offer. Gratiano keeps up the 'Daniel' comparison, more and more offensively.

Shylock, having realised that he has lost the legal battle, turns to leave the court, but Portia has not finished with him yet and now recites another enactment of the law of Venice. This ensures that any person found guilty of threatening the life of a citizen shall forfeit half his goods to his intended victim, the other half to the State, and stand subject to a ducal sentence of death. Gratiano crows over this last straw which completes Shylock's destruction and, when Portia forces him to his knees to beg for the Duke's mercy, Gratiano, showing none, tells him to hang himself.

The Duke immediately gives Shylock his life but confirms Portia's other findings. The defeated Shylock now offers his life since he has been stripped of his livelihood (his means of usury and his capital assets) which for him is the same as being dead. Gratiano cuts in again with the offer of a rope. Antonio returns half of Shylock's assets to him but proposes to take the other half to give to 'his son Lorenzo and his daughter' (389).

Shylock is dealt one final blow. In return for being allowed to retain half his capital, he must become a convert to Christianity and leave a will bequeathing all he dies possessed of to Lorenzo and Jessica. The Duke then threatens him, saying that unless he agrees he will be subject to the ducal prerogative and receive a death sentence after all. Shylock has no choice but to accept these conditions and says 'I am content' (293), leaving the court to the accompaniment of a final blast from Gratiano.

Portia departs hurriedly for Padua but is delayed by Bassanio, who offers a fee for her legal services. She wants no fee, but Bassanio insists. Finally she is persuaded to accept his glove, and, after some argument and overcoming an understandably weak defence on his part, secures his ring, which the audience realises is Portia's own ring, which Bassanio had sworn never to give up.

Commentary

Trial scenes are the very stuff of drama and because of its nature this one is often referred to as the crisis of *The Merchant*, though in fact crisis was reached, as has been pointed out, at III.ii. One must guard against analysing it as though it were an actual trial, representing what might go on in a courtroom. It is a piece of the play and is only to be considered in context. In real life Portia's methods would make a modern lawyer frown and Shylock would have been offered a counsel of his own to advise him and counter Portia's methods of entrapment. The whole court from the Duke downwards is clearly biased against Shylock. This is the effect Shakespeare wishes to create on the stage and we are not expected to analyse it as a justice of appeal might.

Another deliberate stage effect comes in Portia's 'mercy' speech, which is really aimed at the audience. Its dramatic purpose is to draw the line between Christian charity and Jewish vendetta. Though impressively wrought of finely-balanced counterpoint phrases its sentiments originate in the common stock of Christian moral sentiment and are not to be viewed as a serious attempt to persuade Shylock to take the advice of the Beatitudes. It has to be seen to be ineffective, failing to shame Shylock into complying with New Testament humanitarian principles to which he does not subscribe. The crucial word is 'strain'd', associating with Shylock's 'compulsion' (182). In mercy there is no coercion, but nor does it percolate in drops from heaven, like 'gentle rain'.

The focus of the action is Shylock's granite personality and his pride before his fall, though one might conclude that it is not so much a 'fall' as a 'push'. His liability to error and obsession, what the Greeks called *hamartia*, has consistently misled him and is dragging him to the brink of death. This is his tragedy but he does not die physically as he would in a full-blown tragedy. His punishment is that he survives, humiliated, but not because of his financial loss. The court's ruling against him is not as harsh as it seems at first, since he does retain half his goods. His moment of truth has come. He now knows that suffering is indeed the badge of all his tribe and that he must abandon his attempt to change the way of a world which has in his view penalised him because he is a Jew. This is his justification for committing murder, regarded in the Old Testament and according to Mosaic Law as the worst human crime, in settlement of a money debt.

Nevertheless, unpleasant though he has been to others, Shylock is now the underdog, a type which usually attracts pity from an English audience, though such pity may be of the 'there but for the grace of God go I' variety, a view encouraged by the play's emphasis on chance. Shylock implies in defeat a warning not to surrender to fanatical hatred or unquenchable thirst for revenge, irrespective of justification, and at this final stage is almost dehumanised, like the defeated figure of Vice in a fifteenth-century morality play, though Shakespeare never lets him lose human appeal completely. The ancient Chinese proverb about digging two graves, one for your enemy, one for yourself, is illustrated by Shylock's fate.

The process of his collapse is well marked in the text (313, 335, 341, 344–5), but the actual stripping away of the last shreds of his dignity occurs during Portia's reading of the enactment, commencing with 'Tarry Jew!'. This is a challenge to the actor's powers of communication, which must range from bluster at 344–5 to abject surrender to the command 'Down therefore, and beg mercy of the Duke' at 362.

Yet Shylock still has farther to fall. His life is without meaning since his occupation has gone. For a man like him this is spiritual death. Antonio's offer to restore half his goods is generous, since we know that the merchant thinks he is no longer rich, but such a gesture reduces Shylock still further until, with characteristic stolidity in the face of fate, he summons up his feeble reserves and answers 'I am content', an irony, since it cannot possibly be the truth.

The tone of the actor's delivery of these three words may vary from complete surrender to impassive contempt, as though Shylock were thinking, 'What can an honest man expect from you Christians, full of tricks as you are'? The audience has witnessed a reversal of roles, whereby the apparent winner becomes the loser. In *Hamlet* there is a reference to the engineer being 'hoist with his own petard', that is, caught in a self-made trap intended for somebody else.

Shylock's sharpening of his knife may now be seen as farcical, but only in retrospect. Farce is the basis of the clown's art, comic near-disaster, a teetering on the very edge of the abyss but never quite overbalancing, ridiculous but sad, making the crowd feel superior and at the same time sorry for this victim of his own stupidity. To be successful on the stage the conclusion of this scene requires that the Christians be not completely triumphant, but rather to reveal (in some individuals at least) an element of shame.

Shylock's defeat thus attains a degree of emotional intensity not found in other early comedies and this goes some way to explain why early eighteenth-century theatre-managers preferred to leave out much of the rest of the action. The lighter episodes which follow were thought to provide too much of an anti-climax. Nowadays we believe that they were wrong. Shakespeare, clearly realising this danger, effected a slow transition from the trial to the magic atmosphere of Belmont. The ring episode draws the audience away from the conflict of litigation and back into peaceful Belmont, and extends into Scene ii, before we have quite finished with Shylock. To end with Shylock's exit would have been too abrupt, so Shakespeare gives the tragic feelings evoked in the audience time to mellow and soften, so that they may realise that complete catastrophe has been averted and be prepared for the final resolution.

Act IV, Scene ii

Summary
In this intermission of 20 lines the disguised Portia and Nerissa conclude their business with Shylock and plan to be back in Belmont a day ahead of their unsuspecting husbands. Gratiano appears with the ring for Portia, addressing her as 'Fair sir' and we learn that Nerissa intends to play a similar trick on Gratiano with whom she goes off to deliver the deed of gift for Shylock's signature.

Commentary
The brief action extends the ring joke to include Gratiano and Nerissa, in a predictable parallel pattern characteristic of Shakespeare's earliest comedies such as *Love's Labours Lost* and *Two*

Gentlemen of Verona wherein items tend to go in pairs, an inheritance from the Roman comedians Plautus and Terence. The comic spirit is again afoot, though the memory of Shylock's defeat is still kept alive in Portia's instructions to Nerissa and her reference to Lorenzo's coming pleasure when he learns of his gain by the terms of the deed of gift.

Act V, Scene i

Summary
Lorenzo and Jessica open with an exchange regarding the pleasant balmy climate in terms of allusions to separated Greek lovers. A messenger interrupts them to bring the news that Portia is on the way back to Belmont from what they believe was her seclusion at the nearby monastery. Launcelot enters noisily to predict Bassanio's arrival with good news. The air is vibrant with music and the lovers settle down to await the return of the others.

Portia and Nerissa, now undisguised, are welcomed home and we are told of their husbands' impending arrival, which is announced by a trumpet-call. Bassanio, Antonio, Gratiano and their followers come in to begin a light-hearted episode based on the ring-token exchange. The comedy develops as the husbands try to account for the loss of their wedding rings, but their explanations are unconvincing. Eventually Portia and Nerissa reveal the truth about their activities in Venice.

Portia tells Antonio the good news that three of his ships are safe. This is paralleled when Nerissa informs Lorenzo and Jessica of their inheritance from Shylock's deed of gift. The play ends with Lorenzo's thanks to Portia and Nerissa for their efforts at the trial. Portia promises to explain all and Gratiano concludes the action with a ribald comment on the guarantee of his future good conduct.

Commentary
In this act Shakespeare shows his mastery of stagecraft. He has to banish the memory of Shylock's alien world and bring back romance. He does it slowly, by describing moonlight, stars in the heavens and the retreat of darkness, and above all by setting the scene to 'the sounds of music'. This is true poetic drama. Its effect on the modern stage can be overwhelming.

Throughout the act the day dawns. Starting with 'The moon shines bright. In such a night as this . . . ', followed by ten repetitions of 'night' in twenty-five lines, the poet gradually unfolds the change from darkness to light, until by line 295 it is 'almost morning'. 'Shadow', 'break of day', 'morning', 'wake', 'light a candle', 'still dark' and finally 'day breaks', unfold the cyclical change from moonlight to morning light, impossible to suggest by artificial means at an afternoon performance in the Elizabethan playhouse. This dense texture is exemplified in Portia's greeting to her newly-returned husband:

> Let me give light but let me not be light,
> For a light wife doth make a heavy husband, (129–30)

Shakespeare cannot resist a return to his earlier punning style but here it serves to intensify his main emphasis on light as opposed to darkness, one of the most frequently used contrasts in all literature and familiar to all who know the opening of the Old Testament Book of Genesis.

This Act has survived editorial urges to divide it into more than one scene, though the mood changes abruptly at line 126 when Bassanio, Antonio and their followers enter. Until then music affects the atmosphere. It is on the surface a happy one but shadows of the past still remain and their hopes for a bright future may not be altogether well founded in view of the revealed failings of the characters. Although this is Belmont, the odour of Venice is still present because all the main characters except Shylock come on stage. He himself has no place there, though we are twice reminded of him, by Lorenzo at line 17 and Nerissa at line 292. Antonio is also out of his element, though he is physically present.

The first example given of relationships between lovers which Shakespeare later made the subject of a complete play, is that of Troilus and Cressida, but there is irony here since Cressida broke her promise of fidelity to Troilus. The second, of Pyramus and Thisbe, he had already satirised in *A Midsummer Night's Dream*, but the original story ends tragically in the same manner as *Romeo and Juliet*. The Dido and Aeneas and the Medea stories both concern desertion and abandonment. The dialogue repetition of 'In such a night' draws attention to the contrast between the romantic, moonlit setting and these betrayed and betraying lovers whose relationships, like all human bonds, are unstable.

Lorenzo's sudden change to the personal (16) brings his own doubts to the surface. 'Steal' (17) and 'stealing' (19) carry three different meanings while 'unthrift' (18) recalls Jessica's Genoan spending-spree, mentioned by Tubal at III.i.112–3. Her prodigality is now seen by, or at least offered to the audience in a more favourable light as a generous fault, a forgiveable excess after Shylock's 'unthrif-tiness'. It qualifies her for continued residence in Belmont, where Venetian tight-fistedness is unknown.

'Your mistress' (66) is Portia, not Jessica, whose response 'I am never merry when I hear sweet music' (69) attracts Lorenzo's attention back to herself. Lorenzo thinks that this shows her sensitivity to its power, which plumbs depths beyond ordinary day-to-day experience, a flattering explanation such as one might expect from a lover, since

Jessica does not strike one as being particularly sensitive. Jessica's comment may be interpreted as a sign of irritation that his attention has strayed from her to the returning Portia. Her language has a practical ring and she is clearly the dominant partner, self-centred and determined to win, even in a light exchange of 'In such a night' illustrations!

The effect of the music in performance is obviously diminished for the reader of the text. After Capell's 1766 stage directions the musicians in the gallery above were made visible to the audience at line 65 and Lorenzo exhorts them to 'wake Diana' whom, as goddess of the moon, he had identified with the moonlight asleep. The use of 'touches' (67) suggests delicacy of note. In response to Jessica's gloom he calls up an image of how a 'wanton' or unbroken herd of young horses can be calmed by a musical note, and refers to Orpheus, whose musical gift enabled him to charm even the most unfeeling person.

The last six lines remind us of Shylock even in the midst of the romantic atmosphere, for they conjure up the image of a knave, capable of dark deeds, betrayal, acts of plunder, with 'affections' (appetites) 'dark as Erebus' (the road to Hades, the dull underworld of the Greeks). Lorenzo's reference to the untrustworthiness of the unmusical man (83–8) may be related to his own memory of Shylock's opinion of the sounds he heard coming from the masque.

The power of music to weaken human resolution was remarked upon by many Tudor writers on education and government after Sir Thomas Elyot, in his *Book Named the Governor* (1531), advised his readers that it ought to be guarded against. Lorenzo is trying to make time stand still, all human conflict resolved. Harmony flows in with the moonlight as he wonders at the marvel of the heavens, regretting that the music of the spheres, the chord of perfection, is inaudible to corruptible human beings. So he orders the musicians to play inside Portia's palace when he learns that she will soon be back from what he believes to be her monastic retreat. Jessica is much more of a realist, cynical, unsentimental and distrustful of anything that is not material, and this quality, well established in earlier scenes, lingers on, though she does not speak after line 69. Portia and Nerissa, who enter on the phrase 'Mark the music' are impressed by the playing, but neither subdued nor entranced, and their exchange is practical in content.

The metaphor of the moonlight sleeping on the bank reveals Lorenzo's hidden poetic character to Jessica. He draws her eye to the night sky and tries, without apparent success, to make her see its beauty, inlaid with bright golden 'patens' or tiles and every orb or star moving in its own sphere. Until Milton's time poets kept this ancient Ptolemaic concept of the universe alive, though astronomers no longer accepted it. The muddy vesture of 'decay' is a metaphor for the body which has changed, that is, become corrupted. According to the theologians' doctrine of original sin, material change was the sure mark of evil.

When Portia returns to Belmont with Nerissa, they see from afar a candle burning in the hall, a light in the darkness which she likens to 'a good deed in a naughty world' (91), a reference to her own activities in Venice. A former Poet Laureate, John Masefield, thought that this incident was 'full of a naturalness that makes beauty quick in the heart'. The delicate atmosphere of the moonlight scene is gradually dissipated as Portia re-establishes her governance in Belmont and disappears entirely when the music stops, a trumpet sounds and the men return from Venice.

The near-quarrel between Portia and Bassanio is a stylistic trick, sometimes called a 'tracer', and really a take-off of the kind of arguments enjoyed by mediaeval students training in Aristotelian logic. The repetition of 'ring' (over a score of times between line 147 and 259) is a verbal link forged in a chain of causal statements (193–208) making slow progress but building up a sequence which hammers relentlessly on towards a conclusion which finally makes the position crystal-clear. The audience anticipates this inevitable conclusion, when Portia triumphs over her errant husband.

The rest of the scene gathers the threads. Antonio is little more than a bystander, with only eleven lines, and completely dependent on Portia. He has been rescued from the traps of Venice but his despondency trails him since he does not yet know that half his fleet is safe. Although Lorenzo is the first to hear that good news is on its way it is Portia who actually delivers it to Antonio, at the same time that she reveals her dual personality. We are not told how she came by this intelligence. The merchant's acting as surety for the ring is presumably meant to impress upon the audience that Bassanio will never give it up a second time.

Like Bassanio and Gratiano, Antonio has the female sex to thank for his second chance and Shakespeare leaves the audience convinced that fortune and circumstance as well as the 'fatal flaw' determine whether an outcome is tragic or not. The uneasiness which marks the darker comedies, such as As You Like It and Twelfth Night, is detectable in this final act, though it comes from the flawed characters themselves rather than from the story, which appears to end happily.

Though Antonio turns up in Belmont at the end of the play, this merchant–venturer with his ships and his commercial liabilities does not fit in there. His last words concern his ship and we are left in no doubt as to his eventual return to his normal habitat, Venice and the Rialto, whereas the others may continue to disport themselves in the peace of Belmont. The business of making a living and the realm of fancy are incompatible and the former makes so many inroads into the latter as to leave very little that is fanciful at the end of the play.

4 THEMES AND ISSUES

4.1 JUSTICE AND JUDGEMENT

One of the most powerful themes in *The Merchant* is that of justice, fair-dealing among men, giving people their due entitlements, a question not always settled satisfactorily in courts of law and involving the natural rights of the individual in society. Different codes of law prescribe different patterns of justice, but what happens when two such codes conflict? Can they both be 'right'? In a Christian–Gentile society, like Venice, has Shylock's Old Testament code any validity? How far has the Duke's court moral, as distinct from legal, jurisdiction in such a case? The play poses many such questions and leaves the audience to ponder over them, but Shakespeare is not to be treated like a textbook on social philosophy and one must never forget that he was writing a play for his own generation.

Nevertheless, though to claim first that *The Merchant of Venice* deals with types of judgement and second that this is the play's only really important theme may lead one away from consideration of it as successful theatre, these generalisations are not far from the truth. The justice theme *is* central and other issues are related to it, for every voluntary human action is a matter of choice, involving personal judgement. The trial scene represents appeal to a human code of justice and the various forms it may take even within the law's statutes, showing that judgement, as distinct from justice, is relative and dependent upon who is judging and who is being judged.

Ideal justice has always been sought from the time of the Greek philosopher Plato. The Greeks found it in 'natural law', the ideal of one supreme moral law thought to be reflected, though faintly, in surviving human codes of conduct. The Roman Law of Nations evolved out of this natural law and the Venetian law (that is, the Christian authority) maintained the ideal so far as it could be realised in practice consistent with the 'letter' of the law as it was written down. In theory the aim of the Duke's court was to achieve Greek justice tempered with Christian mercy.

In his *Republic* Plato had inquired into the nature of justice in Athenian society. The ideal, he argued, was laid up in heaven, but in practice had to be interpreted as giving each man what was due to him: his 'just deserts' as we say. Shylock has his own notion of his due and believes in the letter of the law, the written law, as his own religion dictated it. He is far more of a moral idealist than any of the Venetian Christians and is strict in his interpretation of the rules as he understands them. His 'scales of justice' are there to weigh the flesh.

The justice theme attracted several of the contemporaries of Shakespeare, who later dramatised it in *Measure For Measure*, notably Edmund Spenser, who devoted Book V of his heroic epic *The Faerie Queene* to it and Sir Francis Bacon, who wrote a famous essay, *Of Justice*. *The Merchant* implies a fundamental question, namely, who or what brings about the best judgement? Should it be a human, fallible judge weighing the evidence?. Or the skill of trained lawyers, looking for legal loopholes? Is there such a thing as a 'just' revenge, taking an eye for an eye, or should decisions involving punishment always be weighed against a set of moral–religious assumptions about 'mercy', such as Greeks, Romans and Christians professed to honour? It is worth pointing out that his religion allowed a Jew to be merciful too, but only if he himself chose. Viewed in this light, the prerogative of mercy was entirely Shylock's and thus for a professedly Christian court to instruct Shylock to show mercy was in the Jew's eyes an impertinence.

At first Portia seeks to represent the Christian tradition, but finding that it does not work in practice, she falls back on legal tactics which her untrained opponent has not thought of. Shylock demands judgement 'by the book' and he gets it, though not in the way he expects. The Duke himself is by no means an impartial judge and even threatens to go back on his pardon to Shylock. Antonio's intercession in mitigation of the sentence passed on Shylock is only relatively 'merciful' and we may even think it contains an element of vindictiveness. Its chief beneficiaries are Lorenzo and Jessica, whose claim is dubious, since their present happiness has been made possible by illicit means. Antonio's other condition, involving conversion to Christianity, was the only alternative to deportation in Shakespeare's day, so may even be considered a kindness.

We are left to decide for ourselves whether we have seen justice, mercy, justice tempered with mercy or a considerable degree of injustice. If one recalls their behaviour towards others, certain of the Christian characters, including Lorenzo, Gratiano and Bassanio himself, appear to get far more than they deserve. Antonio is a good Christian ('a kinder gentleman treads not the earth', according to Salerio) and therefore committed to loving his neighbour, though his charity fails when that neighbour is Shylock, a human being like himself, but a Jew; so perhaps Antonio does merit a lesson, albeit not such a painful one. Gratiano is not very gracious, while Lorenzo is really rather a sneaky fellow and Bassanio is not wholly admirable. Yet their fortunes end happily.

4.2 APPEARANCE AND REALITY

This was a favourite subject of Renaissance philosophers and derived from the Platonic theory of knowledge, which held that true things were stored in heaven and that on earth all that could be perceived was a necessarily misleading reflection. They called it 'accident [or shadow] and substance' and held that the source of man's misery lay in his inability to perceive the truth directly and thus to make correct choices. Such inescapable irony inspired Shakespeare's tragic mood and *The Merchant of Venice* is in some respects a precursor of the so-called 'dark comedies' which harped on this theme. It bodies forth numerous examples of the dangers of judging by appearances and of the intricate deceptions through which the imperfections of human society betray themselves.

Apart from the simple stage device of disguise which can be protective as well as deceptive (as in the case of Jessica), one obvious sign of betrayal is deliberate misdirection by words, that is, telling lies or hypocrisy. Of the main characters, only Shylock reveals to the audience (if not always to others on the stage) what is really in his mind and may therefore be judged by what he says. There is a kind of innocence about him and in the hands of the Christians he becomes a lamb led to the slaughter. It is they who have made the Jew what he becomes (a revenger, as he admits himself at III.i). Portia's contempt for her princely suitors is concealed in their presence while Bassanio's gold-digging motives for marriage are more pressing than the romantic love he professes; much of his earlier conversation with Portia is the preliminary light talk expected of a courtly lover, a style she recognises, and a mild, comic form of hypocrisy.

Predictably, Bassanio and Gratiano do not long resist the moral pressure that urges them to give up their wedding rings. Jessica's betrayal of family ties, the theft of her father's valuables and her tendency to conceal her thoughts even from her lover denotes a great capacity for dissembling. Antonio's strong sense of Christian charity deserts him when he confronts Shylock in the Rialto and though he seems to show a more consistent and transparent personality than his friends he remains something of an enigma.

The gold and silver casket device symbolises the treachery of earthly appearances, summed up in Bassanio's speech at III.ii.73ff, which looks forward to the deceptive character of the law as it is portrayed in IV.i. Though Portia's fine sentiments about 'the quality of mercy' sound magnificent they have no effect on Shylock, who does not subscribe to her religious moral code. At first Portia appears to uphold Shylock's case but her support is not what it seems, since she has studied the 'fine print' in the bond and perceived flaws in the agreement. It is not clear whether or not Portia is a 'genuine' Doctor of Laws in spite of her testimonial from Padua. Nerissa is certainly no lawyer's clerk.

In Christian eyes the Duke's decision may appear to grant the Jew licence to commit murder but Shylock interprets the ruling enthusiastically, welcoming it as a manifestation of perfect justice according to Venetian, that is, 'Christian' law. Portia's expert advocacy seems to him to have legally sanctioned Jewish vengeance, in denial of the Pauline dictum that it belongs to God alone to repay worldly transgressors in kind. The irony of such a situation was later to be revealed in *Hamlet*.

4.3 TYPES OF LOVE

The Greeks had different words for different kinds of love, but the English language is impoverished in this respect. 'Love' is here associated with both emotional and material attachments and the behaviour of the principal characters makes it clear that the first was likely to be short-lived without the second, though both are subject to change. The well-known line in *A Midsummer Night's Dream* (V.i.7) – 'the lunatic, the lover and the poet are of imagination all compact' – likening love to madness, is completely irrelevant in *The Merchant*, for there is nothing of insanity in the love relations of these Venetians.

Like *Twelfth Night*, this play portrays types of love, but in *The Merchant of Venice* material acquisition, born of covetousness or avarice is always present. The marriages in the play cannot be separated from material values and the implication is that some things should not be bought. However, although money is less important than love and friendship the plot shows that whenever romantic love with its promises of undying fidelity and its aura of starry-eyed idealism moves towards marriage it is subject to social pressure exerted by the pressing need for financial security.

(a) Money

Looming large throughout the action is this age-old symbol of material security, money, the power of the purse, upon which the life of Venice and her merchants depends. This is shown by three examples: (1) Antonio's wealth disappears with the apparent loss of his ships, and he cannot pay his debt to Shylock, a failure which seems to be leading him to death. On the restoration of his fortune, Antonio resumes his former existence, his problems solved by the power of gold. (2) Money is shown to be a good thing for Jew as well as Christian. Shylock relies on it for his continued welfare. We hear him mention 'ducats' and the name of his daughter in the same breath and the coin soon threatens to take precedence. When he loses his capital assets his life is finished. He is a widower, his daughter has gone, his religion has been stripped from him. He has nothing left and is even in debt to Tubal from whom he presumably borrowed the money for Antonio (I.iii.58–9). (3) Bassanio is content to rely, first on borrowing, then on gambling his friend's money to secure marriage to a rich lady, while the elopement of Lorenzo and Jessica is made possible by stolen money and jewellery.

Many critics have pointed out the connection between love and money-lending in the play. This is several times reiterated in the casket scene, when Bassanio talks of coming 'by note' (III.i.135). 'Note' meant bill in commercial language. Bassanio's love is always described in this terminology and there are many such references. His first reason for seeking Portia's hand is to clear his debts (I.iii.135) and this impression of his aims endures in spite of his later professions of love. His talk is punctuated with words of material valuation. The same is true of Portia's response to his successful choice (at III, ii 149–60), though she, already well endowed with the world's goods, is thinking of another kind of wealth, made up of love and honour. In *Romeo and Juliet*, love is likewise seen as a form of wealth to be discussed in appropriate banking terminology.

For the late mediaeval aristocracy marriage concerned both love *and* money and for the Elizabethan upper classes to wed for love alone was to give in to a 'dangerous' emotion (using *danger* here in its older sense of illicit entrapment). Richly endowed wedlock was considered to be one of life's more desirable rewards and its recipients were envied by the less fortunate. It follows that the fine words which embellished courtship were known to be ephemeral things, passing fancies suited to the conduct of *fin amour* (upper-class 'refined' love).

Marriage, still referred to as a 'bond', was business. In mediaeval times the cementing of family and territorial ties was a matter of money and property and for the emerging middle classes in the sixteenth century this was still largely true. Romantic notions of marriage as an end in life were to be understood by an Elizabethan audience as a possible source of irony. The lovers in Belmont and Venice would thus be expected to put themselves and their own material necessities first and would be thought fools if they did not. The lottery is a dramatic device through which the practical motives of all the suitors, as distinct from their amorous professions, are revealed and Jessica's arrangements to provide herself with a 'dowry' have therefore to be considered in context, ruthless though her action may appear to a modern audience.

(b) Amity

Amity or friendship, in its ancient Greek sense of *philia*, is another kind of love, partaking of a rare virtue much discussed by Elizabethan writers from Elyot onwards. Elyot considered the capacity for amity to be essential in a governor or courtier. It was the subject of Book IV of Spenser's *Faerie Queene* allegory and of one of Bacon's *Essays*. The word as used in *The Merchant of Venice* implies both friendship and respect, and even conveys an extra dimension, involving the feeling Antonio has for Bassanio and which gets him into so much trouble.

Bassanio's love for Portia is qualified by material considerations, since Bassanio becomes rich by marrying her, but sheer physical attraction, called by the Greeks *eros*, is also present. Portia's amity is said by Lorenzo to have divine attributes and she shows that her relationship with Bassanio is based on it as well as on *eros* when she unhesitatingly prepares to aid Antonio. The love of Lorenzo and Jessica, the love of youth, is physical, less mature and completely governed by *eros*, but later marred because it is maintained by theft and made secure socially by the extraction from Shylock of a forced promise of inheritance. Shakespeare nowhere criticises their conduct and leaves it open to the judgement of the audience.

(c) Loyalty

Related to amity is loyalty and its converse. Antonio is loyal to Bassanio and disregards Bassanio's shortcomings when the latter asks for a loan. Bassanio returns this trust when he journeys to Venice immediately after his marrige in response to Antonio's letter of distress. Portia's loyalty to her new husband is immediately extended to his friend Antonio, whom she has never met, and justifies her assumption of the lawyer's mantle. In pursuing his revenge Shylock is loyal to his tribal traditions and Old Testament principles. Conversely, we have disloyalty, on the part of Jessica, who turns her back on religion and family and, less seriously, of Bassanio and Gratiano to Portia and Nerissa in the matter of their solemn promise not to give up the rings. Launcelot's desertion of Shylock's household for Bassanio's may also be placed in this category.

Shylock is a widower whose only love, apart from that for his money, is directed at the memory of his dead wife Leah, who survives in his daughter Jessica. His treatment of Jessica is, however, unloving and she repays him with disloyalty. Shylock has a friend, Tubal, but Tubal carries bad news so gleefully as to make one doubt if their friendship can be much more than a business association based on mutual self-interest. Shylock is isolated, receives no human love and can give none, for his hate has burned up all his emotional reserves.

Thus, if we seek to find 'true' love in this play, we shall discover that it is as elusive as justice.

4.4 HATE AND REVENGE

In contrast to revelations of the various forces required to sustain the complex emotion of love, we encounter the fanged emotion of hate, represented by Shylock, together with the passions of pride and anger, to which, according to Aristotelian psychology, it is also related. Though not a 'healthy' passion, hate was considered by Renaissance dramatists – and philosophers in certain cases, for example, when it involved honour – to qualify as worthy, provided that its pursuit was controlled by reason.

Elizabethan theatre-goers were familiar with the 'hater' figure, but Shakespeare had not so far tried to create a significant malevolent character. Later he was to bring the type to perfection in Othello's enemy Iago. Shylock is not an Iago, concealing his motives. On the contrary, the Jew delights in rubbing salt into his own wound and explaining exactly why he feels as he does about Christians, the old enemies of his tribe, and especially about Antonio, whom he has come to regard as a representative example of the hostile majority. In course of time, the various elements of his hate coalesce into an obsession, focussed on Antonio.

Revenge, in the same category as hate, represented another 'permissible' passion wherein an offended person might take the law into his own hands. For Jews it was under certain circumstances a tribal obligation. Revenge was a common convention of contemporary drama and one of the most frequent of all definable motives to hostile action, but Elizabethan playwrights followed Christian morality, grounded in the text of St Paul's Epistle to the Romans, 12:19, 'Vengeance is mine, saith the Lord, I will repay', which condemned it as an offence against the Almighty. Shakespeare's contemporary Sir Francis Bacon, who, as we have noted, examined many contemporary issues in his essays, defined revenge as 'a kind of wild justice which, the more man's nature runs to, the more ought law to weed it out'.

In this play revenge resides chiefly in the actions of Shylock, who is presented as an embittered victim of ancient racial and religious prejudice and whose attitude to Christians becomes increasingly aggressive. When Antonio asks for a loan he puts himself in Shylock's power. The latter starts exercising this mildly by defending the practice of usury and retelling a story from the Hebrew Old Testament to justify his own money-lending practices (I.iii.73ff), but when his own daughter elopes with a Christian he is gripped by obsessive hatred and determines to destroy Antonio. Jessica's treatment of him is her own personal revenge and contributes powerfully to his destruction, though some might consider that blame for her actions is mitigated by his long-standing domestic tyranny.

4.5 UNITY

The governing idea in classical, mediaeval and renaissance drama is that human life involves a conflict, with good and evil in opposition. Shakespeare mingled good and evil in one individual and we hardly ever encounter a 'pure' example of either in his plays. Concentration is on 'character' or 'type' and Shakespeare enlarges our minds by making us identify ourselves with the character in question, even when he or she represents the sort of person whom in real life we would dislike. The playwright forces us to ask the question 'Am I too narrow?' Life as projected on his stage is endowed with a fresh significance and in this way we learn how it is that pain as well as pleasure can make it worth living.

The Elizabethan dramatist's ordering of his chosen situation, though conceived nearly four centuries ago, seems in many instances to give satisfaction by offering a solution to our own contemporary problems. Even when that situation is appalling we derive from it what the Greek philosopher Aristotle referred to as 'a peculiar pleasure'. This comes in part from the play's unity.

To understand a Shakespeare play, one must discover the items unifying the various actions. The dramatist has created an orderly view of life as a unity and not as a chaos of disconnected events as we are likely to see it. Shakespeare's plays effect the illusion of perceiving a small part of real life as a whole but it must be remembered that his presentation is *all* illusion, not reality, and that although his characters seem to be human beings like ourselves they are really contrived in order to reveal creation as orderly, not chaotic.

Many Shakespeare scholars have pointed out that the Shylock story is so powerful as to overshadow the love interest. Because of this the play threatens to split into two pieces, inviting the comment that it is structurally flawed and lacking in this essential unity. 'Structure' refers to the way in which the playwright relates different parts of his work to each other and to the whole action. If one part creates an imbalance the audience is likely to be drawn to concentrate on it and consequently pay less attention to the others. This is a serious complaint and poses problems. Victorian actors from Sir Henry Irving onwards gave Shylock the interpretation they thought best and consigned the love stories to a subordinate position.

Having said this, what of the unity of *The Merchant of Venice*? Where does it reside? Does it even exist? In the play Shakespeare brings together an assortment of elements, the stuff of which both tragedy and comedy are made, with the result that its true subject is hard to define. Indeed it may be proposed that a unity has been formed out of opposites. The earliest critics of Shakespeare, writing in the eighteenth century, held human nature to be a unity binding all people together, but with each person a unique mass of contradictions, and maintained that Shakespeare's genius lay in his unequalled ability to portray this infinite variety with sympathy and understanding. In *Hamlet* Shakespeare said that the actor should 'hold the mirror up to nature'.

On this definition the existence of unity in *The Merchant* or in any other Shakespeare play is not to be doubted. Though they may be an unattractive lot, the humanity of each of the characters is (sometimes painfully) obvious. Yet the outstanding idea running through the action is that of love in many of its aspects – physical, romantic, intellectual, spiritual, material, each important for the attainment of happy marriage and strong enough to survive in the face of opposition. Even Shylock was happily married once and one could argue that his loss of a dear wife has deprived him of the solace of love. As we have observed, the romantic and the serious are bridged by Portia, whose journey to Venice is prompted by the love of a wife for her husband which makes her act in his and consequently in his friend Antonio's interests. The unity of *The Merchant* is perhaps most easily perceived in terms of the many facets and motivations of love.

5 TECHNICAL FEATURES

5.1 LANGUAGE

In real life we get to know people largely by the way they speak and everything that goes to make a stage play, physical activity, gestures, pauses, silences, grows out of or helps the language. This action *is* the language and both major and minor personages in *The Merchant* may be identified by the lines Shakespeare has given them. Shakespeare denotes character through carefully chosen words and repeated images, though he occasionally surprises us, as when Lorenzo, who has hitherto been unimpressive as a speaker, suddenly bursts into magic poetry in Act V.

One eighteenth-century poet, Thomas Gray, said that every word in Shakespeare was a picture. Though this was an exaggeration, Shakespeare's vocabulary and readiness to use words in unexpected ways was typical not only of himself but also of his literary contemporaries, who, fired by a new pride in 'Englishness', shared that delight in verbal experiment characteristic of the Tudors. But Shakespeare greatly surpassed other wizards of words, conferring on the English language additional dimensions, nuances, and extensions of meaning which are hard to convey through dictionary definitions. Although the *Oxford English Dictionary* supplies a wealth of these, sometimes as many as twenty or thirty to explore a single word used by Shakespeare, that word's full significance is often hard to grasp out of the dramatic context.

Once he was established and able to dispense with patronage, Shakespeare aimed to entertain the ordinary man rather than the courtier class. His audiences were not semi-literates ignorant of popular culture but sharp-witted Londoners who had inherited orally the accumulated wealth of European folklore and ancient myth. They were developing a powerfully allusive vocabulary of great flexibility and spoke a rich, bold, direct, expressive English permitting a wealth of irregular usages. (A useful modern comparison is with American

English.) The academic grammarians had not yet been able to freeze it and the over-polishers had not succeeded in making this vital medium insipid. English in Shakespeare's lifetime was a vigorous, unhackneyed idiom ideally suited to the popular stage. The far-reaching influence of Elizabethan theatre ensured that written and spoken versions of English would continue to coincide more closely than is the case with any other European language.

Venice is an apparently safe haven, but the opening talk of shipwrecks and storms sets the tragic mood. The language of the rest of the play 'reverberates', that is to say, it frequently plays on this motif so that the audience is not allowed to forget it. Human life pictured as a voyage beset by tempest was an ancient image from Graeco-Roman epic and the Old Testament. This deliberate echoing is an essential part of Shakespeare's stage technique.

Language is subject to constant change and much of Shakespeare's 25 000-word vocabulary is not well understood today. A large proportion of his words, estimated at about 10 000, have become obsolete or have changed in meaning, but in *The Merchant of Venice* we do not have to interpret a series of obscure, half-hidden hints, understand a string of puns, work out of mass of 'inkhorn' or pedantic coinages from Greek or Latin or puzzle out overwhelming numbers of literary allusions.

Though the text contains a handful of difficult archaisms (*slubber* [treat carelessly] and *peize* [weigh or slow down] are examples) the only truly enigmatic passages are found in the jokes of the Gobbos, since Shakespeare's humour (like our own) tends to be related to topical matters. Moreover, much of his verse in *The Merchant* is unornamented and we are not confronted, as in the earlier plays, with an excess of 'patterned' rhetoric, packed with classical images no longer in common currency. However, the play contains twenty-eight direct allusions to Greek myth. Three of the better-known ones are contained in the 'specimen passage' selected, but unlike Shakespeare's audiences (including the 'groundlings') we are likely to require a reference book to help us interpret them. A succinct account is given in M. M. Badawi's *Background to Shakespeare* (1981).

5.2 DRAMATIC IRONY

Shakespeare employs irony a great deal in his plays. Contrast between appearance and reality is itself a larger irony. The tragic or comic element develops from the subject's ignorance of the reality. He is aware of the contrast but is confident that the appearance *is* only an appearance. Later he finds that he is wrong and is trapped. The audience does not share his ignorance and can see that he is being manipulated by some external force or directing intelligence, described generally as fate or fortune, which simply means 'what happens' – the way things turn out for good or ill. One man's good is likely to be another man's ill.

In this play Antonio is controlled by Shylock, who is in his turn manipulated by Portia. Antonio wants to believe in Shylock's good-will and in the continued safety of his own ships. Shylock too relies on the future but unexpected events change his situation from triumph to near-tragedy. A grasp of what is meant by irony is essential to the appreciation of all three casket scenes, disguises, concealment of motive, collusion, misunderstandings and strong suspicions which are disregarded. The ironic mode lends itself to dramatic performance, for when the playwright takes a detached, elevated view of life, as though he were a master of creation, he tends to induce this essentially cruel world of illusion and impose it, sometimes brutally, upon his audience.

5.3 USE OF RHETORIC AND INFLUENCE OF THE EMBLEM BOOKS

In the longer speeches Shakespeare uses several *tropes* or ornamental devices of rhetoric. Classical rhetoric was the art of speaking well, of persuasive oratory, of mastering the eloquence required of a public speaker or advocate. The Greeks gave these devices distinguishing names (for example, *metonymy, synecdoche, periphrasis, hyperbole, catachresis*) and rhetoric was taught as an accomplishment which could be acquired by studying and practising their use. It was one of the basic subjects in the mediaeval scholastic curriculum and an educated Venetian like Bassanio would have been competent in it.

One interesting example occurs at III.ii.85: 'beards of Hercules and frowning Mars'. This is synecdoche (either substitution of the part for a whole or the whole put in place of one of its parts). Likenesses of Greek gods based upon such conventions were pictured in contemporary emblem books. These became the main source of aesthetic delight after the 1540s, when Puritan opposition put an end to public displays of art. Increased attraction of poets and playwrights to these devices was in some measure due to the non-availability of actual pictorial images. Works like Spenser's *Faerie Queene*, described by a French critic, Emile Legouis, as 'a gallery of pictures', were inspired by the dearth of art objects upon which the ordinary man could feast his eyes. Elizabethan enthusiasm for theatrical spectacle and the rapid development of 'poetic' drama owes a great deal to the negative effects of this crudely destructive manifestation of puritanism. The ingenuity with which Shakespeare made word-pictures a substitute for stage action is without parallel.

5.4 STAGECRAFT

From *The Merchant of Venice* Shakespeare's immense dramatic skills can be clearly illustrated. Gratiano's speech in I.i, Shylock's at I.iii, Bassanio's at the caskets in III.ii, Portia's initial plea for 'mercy' in Act IV and Lorenzo's 'moonlight' musings in Act V are landmarks, but the playwright holds his audience not only through language but also by rapid changes of setting and by not permitting any one character to hold the stage for long without a rival. He includes three colourful ceremonies in which the casket ritual unrolls and in the trial scene he fills the stage.

The patterned grouping of the characters who contribute to the main actions is easy to detect: (a) Belmont group (Portia, Nerissa, their servants); (b) Venice group (Antonio, Bassanio, Gratiano, Lorenzo, Salerio, Solanio, the two Gobbos, the Duke); (c) Jewish group, Shylock, Tubal, Jessica; (d) princely suitors, Morocco and Arragon. Of these Shylock, Tubal, Salerio and Solanio, the Duke and Old Gobbo appear in Venice only. The princely suitors appear in Belmont only. All the others, including Launcelot Gobbo, appear in both places. The dramatic effect of such a pattern is essentially to isolate Shylock, so that even though the Jew is dominant he is always alone and at bay.

Shakespeare keeps Belmont and Venice apart by showing what Belmont can offer and what Venice lacks, namely, human sympathy. The intangible qualities of Portia's realm are denoted by its devotion to love's dreams, while Venice is solidly 'financial' and concerned only with the material, as the vocabulary of its residents indicates. Although we know that Bassanio will choose the right casket and Shylock lose his bond Shakespeare has to keep up the suspense and he does it by making the audience concentrate on the present, while every now and again reminding them of what may happen later in images of what has happened before. The 'reverberations' of synonyms relating to storms and other recurrent images of insecurity help to maintain associations. No matter how well we may get to know the play, that tension is always there, generated by the slow, remorseless process of the law's workings, the constant reference to chance as a determinant of happiness in life and love and the progress of the suitors towards their inescapable destinies. Though certain scenes in Act II are there to give the impression of haste and confusion the ritual element is powerful throughout.

5.5 STAGING *THE MERCHANT OF VENICE*

The Merchant of Venice is a powerful and enduring human drama which addresses itself as directly to a present-day audience as it must have done to a full house at the Globe in 1598–9. Although probably composed in 1594, the play was not entered in the Register of the Stationers' Company (the only contemporary protection against unauthorised reproduction or 'piracy' of published plays and pamphlets) until 22 July, 1598. There it was listed first as 'a booke of the Merchaunt of Venyce, or otherwise called The Jewe of Venyce' and again (without the second title) on 28 October, 1600. Records of its earliest stagings are scanty. We are informed that *The Merchant* was 'divers times acted' before its first printing in 1600 and given before King James on 10 and 12 January, 1605 but there is no record of other performances during the seventeenth century.

The Merchant, shifting settings between Venice and Belmont, presents no substantial staging problems and could almost be performed 'flat', that is, on one level, with well-timed entrances and exits, occasionally simultaneous, though most producers today prefer to emphasise the contrast between the two worlds by associating Venice with a lower and Belmont with an upper level. There would have to be connecting steps for easy passage from one level to the other so that Portia may make an impressive entrance and Jessica descend from her balcony. For the episode where Jessica calls down to Lorenzo, and the trial scene, with the Duke and his entourage looking down on the rest, the higher level is obviously needed. The three caskets, central to the plot, would have to be concealed and made visible at the appropriate moment by drawing back a curtain.

One point to note is that, since the Elizabethans were given few stage 'props' to stimulate their imaginations, scene-shifting intervals between episodes were not necessary. This makes some difference to modern performance. The advantages of splitting Act V of *The Merchant* into two parts, thus isolating the moonlight scene, and of accelerating the pace of Act II by eliminating intervals between scenes are doubtful though in some places the absence of such divisions does make for greater continuity of action and the impression of breathlessness and haste accompanying the arrangements for Jessica's flight are more easily communicated without artificial breaks. From the eighteenth century onwards short intervals came to be expected because they facilitated movement of stage properties behind a descending curtain. Moreover, Shakespeare provided neither a list of characters nor a statement of location. This information he built into the text, from which his audience soon learned whether the time was day or night, the weather fair or foul, the place Venice or Belmont.

More elaborate visual effects in this play are confined to the princes' processionals, Bassanio's entry to Belmont in III.ii, the ceremonial of the trial and the costuming of the *dramatis personae*. The costumes represent various degrees of affluence, from the extravagantly attired Morocco and Arragon, the richly-accoutred

Duke of Venice and the fashionably turned-out trio, Bassanio, Gratiano and Lorenzo, to the plainly dressed Shylock and Tubal in their dark gaberdines. Portia could appear as a fairy-tale princess in Belmont but in Venice conventionally garbed in her judicial robes, her femininity hidden. It has been suggested rather obscurely (by Wilson Knight in *Principles of Shakespearian Production*, 1949) that her academic dress should be white, since her 'doctorate' is not from Padua as she claims but is really in 'serene Christian wisdom and feminine intuition', to reflect the combination of realism and symbolism that informs this and other plays of Shakespeare.

Disguises do not have to be convincing, though one *émigré* Russian director with a sense of humour, Theodor Komisarjevsky, who worked in England before the Second World War, gave Portia a beard and spectacles and depicted the bewigged judges at the trial as sheep on a painted backcloth. It is well known that all female parts were performed on the Elizabethan stage by boys, presumably with unbroken voices, though the maturity of some of Shakespeare's later heroines makes one wonder how successful this transvestism could have been in practice. Portia, however, is a sufficiently masculine type to be played by a boy. Contemporary audiences were used to this form of deception, and accepted males in female parts.

Music plays an important part in the action of *The Merchant*. Venice has no music except for the noises of the masque with 'the vile squealing of the wry-neck'd fife' audible from the curtained musicians' gallery. In contrast, background melody helps to convey the harmonious atmosphere of Belmont. The gallery also housed the trumpeters sounding the fanfares heralding the entrance of the princely suitors, but the singer who performs while Bassanio is making his choice of casket and the group softly playing the viols and virginals for the romantic moonlight scene might be more effective if concealed. Eighteenth-century editors were responsible for inserting stage directions which brought the latter into full view.

The Merchant contains no supernatural element, no elaborate make-believe (other than the disguises) and no physical violence, but it does include one sure attraction – a trial. It is here that the action reaches its most arresting point. The dramatic element is never more powerful than in a courtroom, with its cut and thrust of legal conflict, especially when death may be the final judgment. Here Portia and Shylock meet for the first and only time, and if Shylock is garbed in black the contrast with a 'white' Portia will be even more marked.

The trial scene is really a play within the play (a device also used in *A Midsummer Night's Dream* and in *Hamlet*) and the tension as the climax of Act IV approaches, with Shylock getting ready to use his sharpened knife and his scales, must have been immensely heightened by the proximity of the audience to the stage action, with the Venetian courtiers looking down 'from heaven upon the place beneath'. This was a phrase which Shakespeare borrowed from the jargon of professional actors who used to call the canopy over the stage 'heaven', while 'the place' was an old term for the playing area.

5.6 CHARACTERISATION

Shylock

Where Shakespeare found the name Shylock is only to be guessed at. It is recorded as a surname in Sussex in the fourteenth century but the Hebrew *shalach* which turns up twice in the Old Testament means 'cormorant', a scavenging sea-bird, and in one of the 'Roman' plays, *Coriolanus*, Shakespeare refers to supporters of usury as 'the cormorant belly'. Assuredly Shylock (whether pronounced conventionally or as 'shee-lock') sounds a suitably euphonious name for this embittered money-lender from the Venetian ghetto, broad target for a battery of prejudices.

This imaginary Jew is unquestionably one of the dramatist's finest creations, open to a range of interpretations from grave to gay, at one extreme the Jewish sufferer and at the other the melodramatic stage Hebrew; a drooping, ill-used victim of circumstances or a grotesque, pathetic near-caricature of the villain, outmanoeuvred and made to look foolish. He is sufficiently heavyweight to affect the stage action even when he is not part of it, like the intruding skeleton at the feast, and in this respect may be likened to Falstaff in Part I of *Henry IV*. As a lender of money at interest, a type derided and disliked by the Elizabethans, he would have also been despised by Shakespeare's audience as an alien and unconverted Jew, in Christian terminology a sinner bound for hell.

Shakespeare was thus creating a massive difficulty for himself, for he could not have chosen a more unlikely source from which to draw upon the audience's sympathy. Later, he was to take a similar dramatic risk when he made Othello, a Moor, the husband of a white girl, Desdemona, and spent the whole of the first act in demonstrating to the audience that their marriage was right. Portia's comments on Morocco's skin colour suggest that Shakespeare was already considering a future play in which such an unlikely marriage actually took place.

Thus branded indelibly as a potential villain, Shylock is soon perceived to be the chief agent in the serious plot. He appears in only five scenes out of twenty, but affects all the characters in Venice and Belmont, though he is met with only in Venice. He determines most of their actions, even in Act V when he is broken in spirit and the stage is relieved of his physical presence. He gives point to the role of Antonio in the drama and brings the others together, though he himself is a creature apart, a personage of rigid convictions and attitudes to life, unable to change.

Shylock may almost be said to dwell in a 'third World', a Jewish annexe observing ancient law and tradition, from which he emerges to do business and which occasionally threatens the other two. Shakespeare conveys this alien influence cleverly, for example, by bringing in Tubal, mentioning Chus, referring to Hebrew customs and especially through Jessica's account of her restricted home-life.

Shylock appears first with Bassanio in I.iii, and departs alone in IV.i. The Irving tradition dressed him in nomadic robes, with a beard and long grey hair and supporting himself on a staff. He announces his crudest dramatic function in an 'aside' meant for the audience as soon as Antonio joins them: 'I hate him for he is a Christian' (I.iii.43) and soon emerges as the villain, constantly making threats and convincing himself that he is returning hate for hate. He first shows his raw intentions at III.i.74–6, when he tells Salerio and Solanio who are baiting him that 'The villainy you teach me I will execute, and it shall go hard but I will better the instruction'. His objection to Antonio's 'lending gratis' is a comic or 'lightweight' justification for Shylock's animosity. The other reasons which he unfolds, his own religious intolerance, inherited feud and Christian hatred of Jews are deadly serious but remote from English experience. However, this threat to be an efficient villain challenges the Christians and defines him more clearly in the eyes of the audience.

It is tempting to take the line of least resistance in judging Shakespeare's intentions and pursue this character down the thorny path of race relations. This would be wrong. If Shakespeare did write this play to attack the Jews, logic informs us that he is also punishing the Moors in *Titus Andronicus*, the Spaniards in *Much Ado About Nothing*, the Italians in *Cymbeline*, the Britons in *King Lear*, the Scots in *Macbeth* and the English in *Richard II*, as the American scholar G. L. Kittredge sarcastically pointed out in the introduction to his 1945 edition of *The Merchant*.

By the same token, our first view of Shakespeare's Jew as a stereotype is misleading, for it soon becomes plain from the text that Shylock is no undiluted villain, in spite of his extreme threats and what the other characters say about him. He makes his plea in two of the five scenes in which he appears, first in I.iii, as noted previously, and again in III.i, when he argues that Jew and Christian share a common humanity and, by the same token, a like need for revenge. Neither argument is fully convincing, the second being particularly specious as he hides his real motives. Although he shows his obsession by claiming the pound of flesh which is legally his without regard to human considerations for preserving life Shylock is, after all, not a Christian. His rights are neither reduced nor necessarily affected by the dictates of a religion based on charity, which enjoined its adherents to love one another, turn the other cheek to an insult and show mercy to enemies. The fact that a verdict for Shylock means physical death for Antonio is a grotesque irony. The Jew is so ruled by the letter of the law and fired by his own hatred that he cannot see farther than the cold-blooded and repulsive act of carving the flesh. He is thus deprived of the humanity he claims.

The man governed by rigid principle was a conventional humorous figure out of classical Greek and Roman comedy. When such a character is wedded to two popular stereotypes, those of the usurer and the unconverted Christian, such a union brings about the creation of a man whose mania unbalances him to such a degree as to render normal relations impossible. Types of obsession rooted in Roman comedy were to become a favourite subject of Shakespeare's near-contemporary Molière (1622–73). In three plays, *L'Avare*, *Le Misanthrope* and *Le Tartuffe* he created respectively Harpagon, with an unremitting concern for money, Alceste, who refused to conform to norms of social politeness and Tartuffe, a religious hypocrite, who loathed religious hypocrisy. Their fate in each case was isolation. Rigidity was stated as the essential source of the comic in an oft-quoted essay (*Le Rire* [On Laughter], 1900) by the French philosopher Henri Bergson.

Shylock's mania is more complex, for though he is miserly and out to make pecuniary profit he is also a devout practitioner of his religion. An important point to note about him is that, like the misanthropic Alceste, he cannot compromise. At IV.i.375-6 he tells the court:

> You take my life
> When you do take the means whereby I live

but when he is both stripped of his assets and forced to become a Christian, he pronounces himself dead. Unlike Malvolio in *Twelfth Night*, he threatens no further revenge, but quietly withdraws, saying that he is 'not well'. Relieved of his ponderous presence, the atmosphere on the stage lightens immediately.

Shylock, inflexible as he is, cannot be a 'developing' character. The Jew of the trial scene has not changed, except in the focus of his hatred, which as time goes by has become more precisely directed at Antonio. If he learns anything, it is that in a Christian world he will always be a loser. His rigidity remains with him to his last exit and whether he is made to slink abjectly out of the courtroom, as in Victorian performances, or to leave with a greater or lesser degree of gathered-up dignity is, as we have noted, a matter for the individual actor to determine.

In the 1830s the actor Charles Kean made the Jew a melodramatic figure whom the audience loved to hate, with gestures of exaggerated humility and marked foreign accent, a two-dimensional type serving a simple dramatic purpose. Shylock was then always unsubtly classed as a figure of comedy, a descendant of the mediaeval stage Vice related to the clown and fulfilling some of the latter's functions. It is tempting (and very easy) for an actor to overdo the cringing, snapping and snarling, and such a crude interpretation is certainly in accord with a straightforward reading. The hard-hearted father, the miserly skinflint and the domestic bully were, as we have noted, stereotypes to which Shakespeare added an extra dimension when he made his tragi-comic villain a Jew. During the Hitler regime, when anti-semitism was part of official German government policy, *The Merchant*, with a Shylock held up to ridicule, was a favourite with audiences, but no interpretation based on such prejudice is likely to find favour nowadays, though its converse, a completely sympathetic portrayal, would be equally distorting.

A 'modernist' view of Shylock (but a mistaken one) passes over his 'Jewish' attributes and regards him as a rebel against Venetian society. Like all rebels, he has a cause and commands a certain following by the audience. Rebellion was then considered a crime against God by the Church and against the King by the State, so that the individual who opposed his will to the King's Law, was also believed to be fighting God's. This was a powerful means of maintaining social stability. Shylock certainly stands for civil law and order, but he cannot possibly be called a rebel. On the contrary, he accepts the law, confident that he can use it to defeat the very adversaries who made that law.

More convincing is the assessment of Shylock as an upright pillar of Jewish society, cynically enduring prejudice and accepting his lot until, one day, his daughter is taken from him with the help of Christians and even married to one. This naturally stirs Shylock's fury and his relentless pursuit of vengeance is motivated not only by his own desire but also by the dictates of his duty as a Jewish paterfamilias. Solanio's report on Shylock's reaction at II.viii.15ff and the latter's numerous references to Jessica's elopement (the last one in an aside during the trial) underline the weight of Jewish family obligations. Solanio plainly does not realise the enormity of what Jessica has done to her father, who then becomes obsessively bent on getting revenge. To be let down by family would be much harder for an orthodox Jew to bear than for a Gentile, and Shakespeare, realising the dramatic potential of such a situation, made Shylock's emotional outburst excessive. Late eighteenth-century critics saw excess of emotion as the trigger of tragic action.

Considered in this light, Shylock conforms in part (but only in part) to the ancient Greek definition of a tragic figure, the man whose destruction is brought about by sheer bad luck, in that he is touched by the one thing which he cannot endure. Shylock is as much a victim of circumstances as, for example, Macbeth, in whose way Fate places motive, means and opportunity to realise his ambition to be king, thus changing him from a heroic warrior to a blood-stained monster. But Shylock is not a 'hero' and he does not die physically. He is simply removed from the scene and does not even become a martyr to his own cause.

The penalties exacted upon him, including even his forced conversion, are not unduly severe and the Duke's prerogative of imposing a capital sentence is not used. The Jew's loss is only the income on half his property; the other half remains his own for his lifetime. What suffers is his pride rather than his pocket and he is allowed to 'fizzle out'. For this leniency he has to thank his hated foe Antonio – a bitter pill for him to swallow. His fate thus verges on the ridiculous, though it does prefigure Shakespeare's tragic vision, and generations of actors from Sir Henry Irving onwards have found that Shakespeare's flexible text allows for a far greater variety of interpretations than the average Elizabethan audience could have contemplated.

Described as a 'tragi-comedy', in the eyes of purists neither one thing nor the other, *The Merchant* partakes of both tears and laughter, but Shylock neither makes us cry nor is he in the least amusing, though he does come to demand our pity. At times he veers very close to farce, a creature poised on the edge of disaster but who never actually topples over into the abyss. Unlike Marlowe's Jew Barabas, who lands in a cauldron of boiling pitch, noisily done to death in the sensational manner beloved of the 'groundlings', Shylock is never subjected to physical punishment. This would have been too crude for Shakespeare, who saw to it that the same audiences who jeered at Barabas were encouraged to extend sympathy to Shylock.

Of all the characters in *The Merchant*, Shylock is the most easily identified by his choice of vocabulary. Shylock's talk is clipped, intense, for the most part eschewing metaphors, gratingly direct and to the point. He is a business man first and foremost and much of his discourse, from his first line in I.iii, refers to money matters. All he says in that scene relates to his own personal situation and his choice of words brings out the tensions which rule him. By the end of Act I we have learned practically all there is to know about Shylock. He speaks in a mixture of verse and prose, but his verse is really prose cut up into lines, blank verse in name only.

His vocabulary and way of making his position clear is frequently coloured by references to animals of low degree (for example, 'rats', 'dogs', 'goats', 'snails', 'asses', 'mules', 'drones', 'monkeys', 'pigs', 'cats', 'wolf', 'wildcat') and his images are often repulsive ('rheum', 'fangs', 'carrion flesh', 'urine', 'gaping pig', 'thieves'). Emotion is caught in material images of usury ('monies', 'ducats', 'usances') and suffering ('sufferance', 'patient shrug'). Imagery is essentially a comparison or visual analogy and those examples associated with Shylock are drawn from common experience, sometimes implying contact with a contemptible object, such as spitting or spurning with the foot. Shylock's granite will is indicated by images denoting the inflexibility of his attitudes before the Venetian court, (IV.i) such as 'stony' (4), 'rigorous', 'obdurate' (8), 'hard', 'harder' (78–9), 'metal', 'axe' (124–5).

The audience's preconceptions regarding Shylock are kept alive by the direct abuse levelled at him by other characters, principally Gratiano, but also by Bassanio, Solanio, Salerio, Antonio, Lorenzo, Launcelot Gobbo and even the Duke. He is called 'villain' (twice), 'dog' (four times), 'devil' or derivatives (thrice), 'wolf' (twice), 'cur' and 'wretch' (once each), 'currish' (twice). Shylock reminds Antonio of occasions when the latter applied offensive names to him, ('misbeliever', 'cut-throat dog', 'cur') and Launcelot Gobbo implies that his master is worse than the fiend. Lorenzo calls him 'faithless', the Duke of Venice prejudges him as an 'inhuman wretch'. However, it must be understood that abuse and name-calling tells us as much, or more, about the abuser as about the abused.

The appellation 'Jew' is used more subtly. At first it is merely descriptive. When Antonio learns that Shylock intends to let him have the money free of interest he suggests that there may be 'much kindness in the Jew', and, as Shylock takes his leave, adds 'gentle Jew' and an ironic play on 'kind', a quality notably absent from their conversation.

At the trial 'Jew' is employed frequently. Portia commences by asking, for purposes of legal identification, 'Is your name Shylock?' but only on one further occasion does she so address him. Throughout her examination she employs the vocative 'Jew!' while Gratiano's five comments during the proceedings endow the word with 'Christian' contempt. Like Launcelot Gobbo with his 'very Jew', Antonio slanders the race in general when he talks of Shylock's 'Jewish heart' (IV.i.80) but other characters confine their examples to Shylock and his fellow-usurer Tubal, whom Solanio sneers at as 'another of the tribe' (III.i.80).

Elsewhere 'Jew' is used to denote the antithesis of Christian and Gentile, and Gratiano compliments Jessica when he makes the pun, 'a gentle and no Jew', while Lorenzo regrets that she is 'issue to a faithless Jew'. Only Shylock himself, by declaring the common humanity of Jew and Christian, unites the two, though he does this only to justify his revenge. His reiterated scorn for Christians is not removed by his forced conversion.

His obsession governs Shylock's anti-Christian outbursts, the first at I.iii.34–9 and again at line 43 when he declares his 'hate'. He never loses an opportunity to use 'Christian' as an adjective of contempt

(I.iii.43, 161; II.v.15, 33; III.i.52, 66–71, 72; III.iii.15; IV.i.294, 296, 317) and the actor can decide how much venom needs to be injected into each delivery. The last example, at IV.1.317:

> Pay the bond thrice
> And let the Christian go

suggests that the Jew, realising that he is losing, cannot bring himself to use the merchant's name, so tongues his religion in a final swirl of hatred.

Shylock reveals that he is something of a scholar, familiar with scripture. He justifies his own lending principles by telling a story from Genesis 30: 25–43, and he is acquainted with the story of Daniel in the Apocrypha, referred to in the Genevan Bible. He can make mistakes though, and 'your prophet the Nazarite' (I.iii.35) should be 'Nazarene', meaning a man from Nazareth. This shows his (or rather Shakespeare's) familiarity with the early Bibles, which confused the two. The *Authorised Version* of 1611, known as the *King James Bible*, was the first to make the distinction.

Portia

Next to Shylock, Portia is the most outstanding personality in the play, a far more imposing figure than one normally finds in romantic comedy. In contrast with his rigidity, she is flexible, changing easily from one identity to another, moving from her soft, cushioned existence in Belmont to the harsh realities of the Venetian legal code and back again with poise and elegance. In Belmont she is a beautiful and worthy wife for royal suitors, in Venice a tough-minded advocate. Described by Morocco as 'this shrine, this mortal-breathing saint', by Arragon as 'my heart's hope', by Lorenzo as endowed with 'god-like amity' and by Bassanio as 'of wondrous virtues', Portia disingenuously tells Bassanio, who has just made his successful choice of casket, that she is herself 'an unlessoned girl, unschooled, unpractised' but, turned into the cunning advocate Balthazar, she becomes a formidable adversary, more than a match for her stony-hearted opponent.

The device of disguise provides Portia with two outward appearances, but the underlying 'characters' are related. The lady of Belmont does not really change more than her apparel to become the advocate Balthazar. Her vocabulary alters as she assumes a tone of legalistic formality, but in both Belmont and Venice her handling of the male sex reveals the same assumption of intellectual superiority and ruthless lack of scruple. The ring incident brings out her cynical view of men, first shown when the shrewd, feline Nerissa names the lottery candidates one by one and listens enthusiastically as her mistress cartoons their personalities in turn. Portia also disparages her two princely suitors, according neither any virtues.

Portia is mature and perhaps 'un-English' in that she does not expect male fidelity, though she would obviously prefer to believe in the possibility of its existence. She is no romantic mistress and enters into the union with Bassanio in a practical spirit, knowing very well that he is a fortune-hunter, accepting his superficial attractions without harbouring illusions. She tells him that she is not in love (III.ii.4), but is ready to settle for him as a husband and hopes he will choose correctly, guided by Love which, in excess, she mistrusts. In her Bassanio has acquired a reliable wife but one who will claim superiority and hold the ascendancy. Lorenzo's heavy compliment, perceiving that Portia has 'a noble and a true conceit / Of god-like amity' (III.iv.2–3) draws from her a rather priggish response commencing 'I never did repent for doing good' (10) and though some critics may see it as part of a 'conflict of the sexes' joke, her threat to deny him marital rights and her echoing of his repetitious protest about the loss of the ring in Act V can equally well be taken as further evidence that Portia has it in her to turn into a shrew.

Of language, Portia has two styles, the Belmontine, which is cynical, witty, sophisticated and familiar, studded with 'conceits', and the Venetian, which is austere, aloof, formal, with discourse related strictly to the facts of the case, her knowledge of the law and the written word. Sometimes they merge, as in her first prose conversation with Nerissa at I.ii. When she deals with Morocco and Arragon in Belmont her tone is legalistic and tending to sarcasm, as it is when she taxes Bassanio with infidelity in the last act. She is not inclined to reveal her intimate self, however, and most of her statements are factual. She ventures into metaphor occasionally, but only in short bursts (for example, III.ii.108ff, when she cannot restrain her relief that Bassanio has made the correct choice of casket).

Her dual personality is reflected in the two styles. Some of the observations made to Nerissa anticipate her courtroom speech, so that the split between the two personalities is not completely out of character — Shakespeare is too skilled a craftsman for that. But no matter where she is, or in what guise, Portia is easy to understand and there is nothing convoluted about her statements.

Nerissa

Portia's maid and loyal confidante, the dark Nerissa is a distinct personality and not just a foil for the 'fair' Portia's wit. She rejects Portia's melancholy pose just as Gratiano rejected Antonio's. Her opinion of men is similar to Portia's and her memory for the latter's past suitors is excellent. In fact it is she who first brings Bassanio to her mistress's attention, and she is quick to seize the opportunity of grabbing Gratiano for a husband, since he falls in love with her romantically, at first sight. She agrees to marry him, but not before she has made Bassanio's success a condition of her own betrothal. Her role in the ring episode increases in dramatic effect as she follows Portia's lead in every respect, even to the half-serious threat to withhold connubial bliss from her husband.

Her talk is inclined to extravagance in Shakespeare's earlier style, which associated plays on words and bawdy talk with lower-life characters like nurses, servants and clowns. Nerissa's marriage to one of the gilded youths of Venice elevates her above her earlier role as lady of the princess's bedchamber and it is misleading to regard her simply as a 'maid' in the modern sense. 'Lady-in-waiting' is a more accurate description.

Antonio

One way of looking at the play is to consider it in terms of its title, with Antonio as the central figure. A popular recast version performed in the eighteenth century used the alternative title *The Jew of Venice*, but Shakespeare called it first *The Merchant of Venice*, indicating Antonio. Yet compared with the others Antonio is so muted as to bring us to the conclusion that there is little to say about him. He enters on a low key and most of what he says is either negative or resigned. He initiates no action and his speeches are with one exception (I.iii.131–7) lacking in animation. To the end he is forbearing and honourable even when contemplating his imminent death.

This is the stuff of which martyrs (or fools) are made. The merchant has nothing of the tragic hero in him. However, he *is* the fountainhead of the action and this may explain Shakespeare's title, though the playwright did not set much store in titles, several of which (for example, *Much Ado About Nothing, As You Like It, Twelfth Night or What You Will*) give no clue as to their subject-matter. Perhaps he simply wanted to avoid using the word 'Jew' and thus inviting superficial comparison with Marlowe.

Antonio is of Shylock's commercial though not his social world and is not a romantic figure at all, in spite of his melancholy posture at the start of the play. With his talk of ships and financial liabilities, he does not fit in at Belmont, though he is washed up there like a castaway in the final episode. Is Antonio, therefore, just an honourable idiot, a kind of comic Othello? His own reckless commercial venture lands him in trouble, but it is Bassanio, his great friend, who exposes him to the usurer. Yet his response to Bassanio's request for funds is immediate, unthinking, open-handed and generous. Bassanio is his friend in need and Antonio does not question his necessity. He feels obliged to help him as he had done in time past.

Antonio's Christian virtue of charity has not been extended to Shylock, however, and he is angered and unrepentant when Shylock reminds him of frequent past insults, including spitting on his clothing – hardly the kind of action expected of a gentleman. Antonio has been brought up to regard Jews as less than human. For him Jews simply do not exist socially, not even an intelligent, scholarly and well-informed one like Shylock, and count for nothing except in business circles, practising their despised trade.

Antonio's place in the simple pattern of action has been described (by a former Poet Laureate, John Masefield) as that of the man of heart as opposed to Shylock the man of brain. He acts according to his passions and does not count possible consequences. Like Shylock, Antonio undergoes no development, except to make a slight gesture of restitution towards his fallen adversary after the trial verdict, though his attitude to Jews stays unaltered. His last words in the play may be contrasted with Shylock's protest at IV.i.375–6. Whereas Shylock fears that he has lost his life and his means Antonio has regained, through Portia, 'life and living' now that he knows his ships are safe. As noted earlier, the ancient classical and biblical image of the vessel threatened by storms and seeking a safe haven was frequently employed in sixteenth-century literature to denote the stressful course of human life at the mercy of fate.

Bassanio

Bassanio is introduced as a shallow type, a flawed knight errant, superficially appealing. Nerissa describes him as 'a scholar and a soldier' (I.ii.119). Ironic misrepresentation of this kind would be in keeping with his revealed character, which is that of a prodigal, a fortune-hunter, an amusing young man about town but hardly a figure to be admired. He is a smooth talker, used to getting what he wants. In spite of their eccentricities Morocco and Arragon seem more reliable than Bassanio. We do not doubt their intention to keep to the conditions attached to a wrong choice. Nevertheless it is Bassanio alone of the named suitors who makes a good impression in advance. He is the most personable of a mediocre lot.

His talk is full of unconscious ironies and contradictions. For example, he rejects gold and silver (III.ii.101–4) but we know that he is hard up. He selects the plainest casket and and when he finds that he has picked the right one, contradicts all he said earlier. He appears to base his selection upon a series of moral judgments (III.ii.73ff) but earlier in the action (I.i.162–4) had told Antonio that Portia is 'a lady richly left', 'fair' and 'of wondrous virtues', obviously the order in which he seems to value her attractions. Bassanio's sentiments reflect the cynicism of a young sophisticate and are best judged as belonging to a stereotype. Their real dramatic function is to relate his choice of the lead casket to the wisdom of not choosing by appearances.

At the same time, his rejection of outward show has to be taken as a sign of maturity – what Shakespeare was to call 'readiness' in *Hamlet* and 'ripeness' in *King Lear*. It is also a symptom of the tragic mood when a man first realises that things are not always what they seem. Bassanio prefigures the Hamlet-type in his resolution to cleave to reality in future. This is irony within irony, since Bassanio is no more a tragic character than Antonio. His sententious musings before the caskets are derived from his 'courtly' pose. Underneath he is concealing his private calculations in an outward show of rhetoric.

Bassanio's loyalty to Antonio is unshaken, though considering his own good fortune he does not have much to lose by backing up the merchant. He responds to Antonio's written entreaty and, now that he is a rich man well able to afford it, makes a grand gesture before the Duke's court, offering to settle his benefactor's debt. He even promises, in suitably impressive language, to sacrifice his own 'flesh, blood, bones and all' but the audience knows that he is unable to rescue Antonio. It is his wife in disguise who can do this. Such self-dramatisation confirms his essential impotence.

On the principle that the devil looks after his own, Bassanio triumphs. He gets his loan, he wins the lady, his material welfare is assured and he joyfully becomes master of Belmont, though we may think that perhaps Venice is really the more suitable place for him and that in his way he is as much a 'merchant' as any of the Venetians. The token of his triumph is Portia's ring, but he puts the wishes of his wife (who he thinks is far distant in Belmont) second to the case-winning lawyer's more immediate pressure and has no choice but to break his vow. His role here is fundamentally that of the deceiving male who is also deceived, a familiar figure in naïve comedy.

Bassanio is thus an unusually elaborate version of the comic 'courtly lover' who leans on others for his own security, profits by accident and comes out smiling without much personal effort. Shakespeare's fine hand has given this character much more depth than such a light leading part usually merits. It is possible for us to accept him for his honourable relations with men while not taking him very seriously in his dealings with women. He falls short of being really likeable, however, and one feels that his friendship is likely to prove costly to the recipient.

Gratiano

Gratiano's is a complex personality. Although his name (which Shakespeare uses in three other plays) suggests the stage Fool, this character is certainly no fool in the sense of being intellectually lacking. Like Bassanio, Gratiano is a young man about town but of a more flamboyant temperament and, like Nerissa, Gratiano soon emerges as a personality in himself, imparting greater solidity to his dramatically more important companion.

He has three main functions: (1) to mark the contrast between the cheerful and the melancholy man in the first scene with Antonio and to voice that dislike of puritanism which Shakespeare consistently shows in other plays; (2) to support Bassanio in his ventures in both Belmont and Venice and (3) to express the common Elizabethan's anti-semitic prejudices, normally latent but quick to rise whenever opportunity presents itself.

Much of what we learn about Gratiano derives from what he says to his friends in I.i – his talkativeness, insensitivity, tendency to hold the floor and his blunt, rough manners, which he claims he can change at will if he is permitted to accompany Bassanio to Belmont. Yet his phrases are polished, his allusions learned and there is more than a suggestion that behind the façade of exuberance his playing of the fool is a mask.

Gratiano's first and longest speech (I.i.79–104) constitutes a rough attack on the melancholic humour possessing Antonio, whereupon Bassanio finds it necessary to assure the merchant that Gratiano is not to be taken seriously though it is clear that beneath his outward show of flippancy he means what he says. His harsher side is revealed more directly at the trial when he acts as a hostile chorus by repeating Shylock's own words and expressing his animosity in direct epithets of abuse. In Act V he returns to his former role. His marriage to Nerissa and his failure to keep his promise to her parallel Bassanio's.

On occasion Gratiano's language can be offensive. His epithets in Act IV when Shylock is present are cruelly and crudely anti-semitic. In Act V Shakespeare lets him have the last (and bawdiest) word in the play, vowing an obscene fidelity to Nerissa, and Gratiano's milder conduct is overshadowed by his sneers at the trial (IV.i.123–6, 128–38, 289–91, 311, 316, 322, 332–3, 339–40, 363–6, 378 and 397–9). His most persistent image recommends Shylock's execution ('the hangman's axe', 'cord', 'halter', 'gallows'), or suicide, a mortal sin ('hang thyself'), and he delights in throwing Shylock's own words back at him (IV.332–3) though Gratiano was not present when Shylock used 'on the hip' (a wrestling term) at I.iii.47.

However, the impression he first makes is one of light-hearted if thick-skinned garrulity and it is not until he refers to Jessica as 'a gentle and no Jew!' (II.vii.51) that Gratiano's darker aspect begins to show. He can make eloquent speeches (I.i.79ff and II.vi.8–19) and his marriage to Nerissa prompts another but more forthright outburst (III.ii.197–208). His colourful speech commencing 'Let me play the fool!' depends on personification and extended simile and is a good example of his chameleon-like capacity to assume different roles. We are never quite sure if in Gratiano's case the reality might not be the appearance and vice versa.

Jessica

The name Jessica appears in Genesis. Jessica is to some extent the conventional runaway bride, escaping from her tyrannical parent, but Shakespeare, probably thinking of Abigail in Marlowe's *The Jew of Malta*, who throws her father's treasure out of the window and also converts to Christianity, gives Jessica extra dimension. Such a character turns up in an Italian *novella* of 1541 (though not as the offspring of a Jewish money-lender) and an English plot of 1580 combines the bond story with the winning of the money-lender's daughter. The ungrateful daughter-type was thus not original to Shakespeare, but in *The Merchant* he fleshes her out far more than any of his predecessors had done.

She is to marry a Christian and is not alienated from the Gentiles, even before her conversion. None of the Christians, not even Gratiano, who calls her 'fair Jessica' (II.v.29) voices any objection to Lorenzo's relationship with her, presumably because she is soon to be converted. Salerio tells Shylock that father and daughter have neither flesh nor blood in common (III.1.41–4), which is another way of saying that she is acceptable into Gentile society.

Jessica is an ambiguous character open to several interpretations. The actress playing the part can present her either as a chip off the old block, a true daughter of her father the Jew, with some of his frustrations and obsessive ruthlessness or as an admirable rebel in love across racial and cultural barriers, though here her conduct towards her parent invites some measure of condemnation.

Jessica is indeed a rebel but her rebellion is domestic, against Shylock and his strictness, not against the alienation of her race. The enormity of what she does to her father is less obvious to a non-Jewish audience, but the more Jessica is regarded as a solid flesh-and-blood personality and not as a romantic lover the less appealing she becomes. She and Lorenzo do not seem to have much in common and she does not appear to share his perceptions of beauty in the moonlight. In Belmont she appears somewhat out of her element.

Her talk is for the most part down-to-earth, directed to imparting information, and Shakespeare raises its level above the domestic only twice in the play, once at III.v.76–86 and again at the beginning of Act V, when she cites Greek myth as elegantly as Lorenzo. Her motives for marriage, (II.iii.20–1) are stated in an order that is severely practical and may be compared to Bassanio's (I.i.162–4).

She leads where Lorenzo follows and at least once (in III.ii.221) seems to have been kept in the background by Shakespeare lest she draw the audience's attention away from the continuing main plot. Here Gratiano refers to the couple as 'Lorenzo and his infidel' though after an interval as 'yond stranger' (238), though he has seen her once before, in poor light, dressed in boy's clothes on the balcony of Shylock's house.

The actions of Jessica serve to retard the pace of the audience's growing antipathy to Shylock and to establish that, so far as the Gentiles are concerned, he does not have the law on his side. The latter fully support Jessica, looking upon her almost as one of themselves, 'a gentle and no Jew', and Shylock's 'gentle daughter', eventually to be imported into Belmont. The otherwise superfluous talk between Launcelot and Jessica in III.v favours her while denigrating her father. Portia's reliance on Jessica, whom she has only just met, as a caretaker for Belmont indicates that Shylock's daugher impressed her as domestically reliable. She had, after all, been her father's housekeeper (II.v.15–16).

Jessica's conduct appears to have some justification, since Shylock is depicted as a domestic tyrant of the old school who frustrates his child's natural desires and does nothing to please her at home. She repays him by robbing him and eloping with a Christian, even becoming converted herself. The selling of her mother's ring denotes Jessica's total rejection of family ties.

Lorenzo

Lorenzo, an introspective young man inclined to pessimism, is the more outwardly sensitive of Bassanio's two bachelor friends and somewhat under Gratiano's thumb (I.i.107). He is close-mouthed, as befits a conventional romantic lover keeping his amour secret. This may be deduced from the fact that although we hear that Launcelot is being used as a go-between to deliver a love-letter to Lorenzo (and from Jessica herself that he has promised to marry her), Lorenzo himself says very little until II.iv. He conceals his intentions from his friends until this scene, when he tells them of the plans for elopement, devised not by himself but by Jessica. His frankness here is inconsistent but serves a dramatic function.

He is brought in at III.iv to convince Portia of Antonio's worthiness and flatters her understanding of what friendship means ('godlike amity'). In III.v Lorenzo is given more to say than might be expected from his earlier reticence, but this is only a 'makeweight' scene contributing little to our knowledge of him. His exchange with Launcelot does show his preference for plain speaking over 'wit', but in the following dialogue with Jessica he shows himself inferior in repartee. However, Lorenzo's rhetorical powers are not revealed until V.i.54–68 and 70–88 when, in his role as perfect courtly lover, he undergoes a magic transformation and utters the finest poetry in the play. Jessica is silenced. Lorenzo appears to be more at home in Belmont than either of the other two husbands, though after line 123 he remains on stage only as a bystander with nothing to say, in keeping with his original subordination to Gratiano. Compared with him Lorenzo is lightly sketched in and leaves an impression of easily-led pliability.

Minor characters

Minor characters, even the walk-on servants given a couple of lines, are not to be regarded simply as wooden 'extras'. They are essential to the play's unity. In *The Merchant* there are nineteen speaking parts. Of these the significant minor characters include Salerio and Solanio, the two Gobbos, Tubal, the Princes of Morocco and Arragon and the Duke of Venice.

Salerio and Solanio

Salerio and Solanio (in some editions joined by a third and superfluous character called Salarino who is given some of their lines) are in Antonio's circle but their association has less intimacy than Bassanio's (see I.i.59–60). They have similar-sounding names and come on stage together or separately in eight scenes as listeners, commentators or messengers and serve to expand the male society surrounding the merchant. As the producer and critic Harley Granville-Barker said, their function is 'to paint Venice for us'. He also remarked that actors cursed them as 'the two worst bores in the whole Shakespeare canon'.

They are associated with revelations about Antonio's ships from I.i to III.i, and act as typically Gentile commentators on Shylock's attitudes to money and his daughter after her flight, adding to the 'hate' picture of Jews – Solanio refers disparagingly to Tubal at III.i.80–2. In III.ii Salerio is a messenger from Antonio and appears in Belmont bringing bad news about the bond, which makes Bassanio confess to Portia that he did not at first tell her the whole truth about himself.

In III.iii Solanio is with Antonio when Shylock arrives. The Jew's obduracy shocks Solanio, who tries to console Antonio with the prediction that the Duke will support Antonio, the common man's reaction to the legal position. At the trial Salerio is a spectator. Solanio is not mentioned and we may ask what has become of him – one of Shakespeare's many unanswerable questions.

The Gobbos

'Gobbo' in Italian means 'hunchbacked' but it was also an English surname, probably a form of 'Job', known in Titchfield, the county seat of Shakespeare's patron, the Earl of Southampton. The Gobbos, father and son, appear together in one scene only (II.ii), when Old Gobbo plays 'stooge' to Launcelot Gobbo's clowning, but the main purpose of the first 33 lines of this scene is to build up our picture of Shylock as a harsh master from whom his servant wishes to escape. Launcelot gives us a 'below stairs' servant's view of Shylock from the Gentile point of view and his language brings together the powerful images of Shylock and the Devil.

Though Jewish master and Gentile servant are seen to be incompatible in II.iii, Launcelot assumes the role of go-between aiding the love-match of Jessica and Lorenzo. The misery of Shylock's domestic household is confirmed to the audience by what Jessica tells him and his reference to this particular Jew as 'sweet' further isolates Shylock. His function thereafter is as a messenger or link, and it is misleading to call him 'a clown'. His exchange with Jessica in III.v could be discarded without great loss and serves merely to separate her further from Shylock. On Lorenzo's entrance, Launcelot turns into a word-quibbler, as Lorenzo points out, the wise fool, like Feste in *Twelfth Night* or Lear's Fool, trying out refined language, but less successfully.

Old Gobbo's appearance serves as further comic relief and he would be dressed eccentrically, speaking in dialect, which on the Tudor stage was a way of indicating rustic ignorance. The humour of II.ii is naïve, based on misunderstandings due to the old man's blindness and inability to identify his own son. When Bassanio enters, Launcelot tries to present his father in the most favourable light. His flattery appears to work as he becomes Bassanio's servant, possibly his official fool, and is given a superior uniform. Launcelot is a multi-purpose character showing a considerable range in speech and action and fitting in everywhere he goes, even appearing at Belmont in Act V in his role as messenger.

Tubal
Tubal (the name comes from Genesis) makes one appearance and lights up Shylock's mixed emotions for the audience. He gives the latter bad news, and seems to delight in Shylock's discomfiture, indicating that he is not so much a real friend as a rich business crony on whom Shylock occasionally relies for his own credit. Tubal is introduced by Solanio as another of 'the tribe' and adds dimension to the money-lender's world. Shylock's earlier reference to him prepares us for his eventual entry. Jessica also mentions him (and another Jew, Chus, who does not appear) at III.ii.286.

Morocco and Arragon
Like all Portia's named suitors, the two princes are distinct types, although we meet only these two besides Bassanio. Morocco is egocentric but in his fashion a man of honour. Like the gold he

chooses, he has a glittering, surface attraction, but soon reveals himself a bore. His boast, associating himself with superior beings of 'a golden mind', is comically ironic since at bottom his valuation of Portia is monetary. His reference to her as an 'angel' (a slang term for a coin) underlines this. His choice of a death's head indicates that he is spiritually dead, as, according to mediaeval theologians following the Pauline–Augustinian prescription, all were dead who pursued the purely material. His eventual exit is dignified and he takes his defeat well.

Arragon, on stage to repeat Morocco's error, appears in one scene only and his name implies his head-in-air pride. Obsessed by rank, he is another who judges by appearances and holds the low peasantry, the barbarous multitude, as he calls the majority, in contempt. He is however an idealist of a sort, seeing himself narcissistically as the vision of human perfection. When he opens the casket his language loses its polish and he suddenly comes down to earth with a realisation of his own stupidity.

The Duke of Venice

We are introduced to the Duke gradually, by references at II.viii, III.ii and III.iii, but do not actually meet him until the trial. We have been warned about his partiality and on stage he shows it from IV.i.3, first by characterising Shylock to Antonio in the most derogatory terms and at line 16 by instructing Shylock that he ought to withdraw his plea on 'humanitarian' grounds. As a judge he is blinkered, unable to see that Shylock's standards are different from his own, and cannot understand the compromise sought by such an interpretation of the law. He is ready to dismiss the court and use his ducal prerogatives to escape his judicial dilemma, but Portia–Balthazar shows him a way out. He pardons Shylock, saying that the Christian spirit is merciful, then threatens to go back on his earlier decision. This Duke–Magistrate figure is more of a one-dimensional 'prop' than the others and his function in the play is mainly to show that the ultimate authority in the practical application of Venetian justice is an uncritical upholder of *status quo*.

6 SPECIMEN CRITICAL ANALYSIS

The Merchant of Venice is not distinguished for its metaphors and is generally written in a plain style including long stretches of prose. The passage chosen has been selected on two main grounds: (1) that it is the dramatic centre and crisis of the play, a point first made by the nineteenth-century critic R. G. Moulton, and (2) that it refers in turn to four of the play's principal themes. It is also one of the more varied to be found in the play and is itself about a choice.

The passage contains a song, a speech by Bassanio and an aside by Portia. Bassanio is trying to make up his mind as to which of the three caskets to open and in doing so touches on the major themes of the play. His talk is audible as a dramatic convention but in realistic terms these are the thoughts going through his mind at the moment of selection, in the manner of a soliloquy.

His musings are preceded by the song, prepared for by a musical introduction commanded by Portia at line 43. This contributes to the atmosphere of expectancy and differs from the two earlier casket scenes, which had no musical accompaniment and lacked the romantic atmosphere of this one.

Music. A song while BASSANIO *comments on the caskets to himself.*

> Tell me where is Fancy bred –
> Or in the heart, or in the head?
> How begot, how nourishèd?
>   Reply, reply.
> It is engendered in the eyes
> With gazing fed, and Fancy dies
> In the cradle where it lies.
> Let us all ring Fancy's knell.   70
> I'll begin it – ding, dong, bell.

ALL   Ding, dong, bell.

BASSANIO   So may the outward shows be least themselves;
The world is still deceived with ornament.
In law, what plea so tainted and corrupt.
But being seasoned with a gracious voice.
Obscures the show of evil? In religion.
What damnèd error but some sober brow
Will bless it and approve it with a text,
Hiding the grossness with fair ornament?   80
There is no vice so simple but assumes
Some mark of virtue on his outward parts.
How many cowards, whose hearts are all as false
As stairs of sand, wear yet upon their chins
The beards of Hercules and frowning Mars,
Who inward searched have livers white as milk?
And these assume but valour's excrement
To render them redoubted. Look on beauty.
And you shall see 'tis purchased by the weight,
Which therein works a miracle in nature,   90
Making them lightest that wear most of it.
So are those crispèd snaky golden locks,
Which make such wanton gambols with the wind
Upon supposèd fairness, often known
To be the dowry of a second head.
The skull that bred them in the sepulchre.
Thus ornament is but the guilèd shore
To a most dangerous sea, the beauteous scarf
Veiling an Indian beauty; in a word,
The seeming truth which cunning times put on   100
To entrap the wisest. Therefore, thou gaudy gold,
Hard food for Midas, I will none of thee;
Nor none of thee, thou pale and common drudge
'Tween man and man. But thou, thou meagre lead
Which rather threaten'st than dost promise aught,
Thy paleness moves me more than eloquence,
And here choose I. Joy be the consequence!

PORTIA   [*Aside*] How all the other passions fleet to air,
As doubtful thoughts, and rash-embraced despair,
And shudd'ring fear, and green-eyed jealousy.   110
O Love, be moderate, allay thy ecstasy,
In measure rain thy joy, scant this excess!
I feel too much thy blessing; make it less
For fear I surfeit. (III.ii.63–114)

The song poses a riddle, an ancient form of entertainment originally
meant for children, and takes the form of question and response.

Fancy is personified and refers here to romantic illusion, originating in the sight of the beloved object. Its words contain early glimmerings of the later Shakespearean tragic mood and are in fact an elegy to Fancy = attraction by outward show, compared with True Love which springs from 'heart' and 'head'. The Greeks placed the appetitive below the intellective power and the Elizabethans accepted this classification, subordinating both to the spiritual. The singer's question reflects a contemporary notion of human development towards the divine, that is to say, away from the senses through the intellect and towards the liberating poetic imagination, a theme which Shakespeare was to pursue in *The Tempest*.

The symbolism is transparent. Fancy is represented in the style of the popular emblem books as a baby, unable to stand up or feed itself and by implication short-lived. The onomatopoeia in 'Ding, dong, bell' would be echoed by the actual tolling of a bell from the musicians' gallery. Since Fancy was thought to lead men and women into judging by appearances and theologians citing the Biblical Fall classed Fancy as 'concupiscence of the eyes', this was a temptation to be guarded against. Considered in terms of the psychology and moral philosophy of the time the song is both a warning and a lesson. Realisation that Fancy must soon die was interpreted by the Elizabethans as an inevitable stage in the maturing process of acquiring 'ripeness', of which human tragedy was an inescapable part. Feste's concluding song in *Twelfth Night* carries a similar message.

Critics have suggested that Bassanio, listening, takes instruction from the singer's end-rhymes (*bred, head, nourishèd*) and draws the conclusion that Portia's portrait must therefore be concealed in the 'lead' casket. This is an appealing argument, but the content of the speech that follows does *not* entitle us to assume that the purpose of the song is to advise him to make a correct choice as Portia wishes. His opening statement (73–4) refers to the caskets and not to the song.

If the caskets are set well apart Bassanio can pace from one to the other as he goes on with his monologue which points in turn to four themes in the play – deception, legal juggling, religious hypocrisy and the elusiveness of truth. In twenty-three lines (74–96) we are presented with a 'parallel' (repeated) structure of several examples conveyed by the methods of rhetoric. His debate consists of a succession of elaborate allusions to deceptions practised (1) in law by skilful oratory (75–7); (2) in religion by distorting scripture (77–80); (3) by vice disguising itself as virtue (81–2); and (4) by natural physical beauty simulated by artificial aids (88–96).

In his denunciation of the untrustworthiness of feminine allurement Bassanio's image of the bewigged head merges into another of death and the tomb. This looks forward to the fury of Hamlet who condemns the female sex in the same terms, but Bassanio's denunciation is restrained. Finally, he rejects all 'ornament' and likens it to the veil of 'an Indian beauty'. 'Indian' or 'Eastern' here means dark-complexioned, then thought inferior to the fair. Nerissa, whose name denotes 'dark', (from the Italian *nero*, meaning black) and who is on stage with Portia, has to be regarded as inferior to her mistress in attraction.

The full significance of 'crispèd snaky golden locks' (92) depends upon a mental process called 'association of ideas' first described by Aristotle. There is no actual connection between snakes and arti-ficially curled golden hair but a ready link is forged by the adjective 'snaky'. The snake has Biblical associations with evil and is here related to gold as an alluring but potentially malign trap, just as beauty 'purchased by the weight' (89) is echoed by 'lightest' (91) implying a 'light' woman, a harlot painted up to entice men. This is an extended comparison in the style of the Homeric simile, wherein one thing is compared to another at length and in detail.

The metaphor calling ornament 'but the guilèd shore / To a most dangerous sea' (97–8) and reminding us of the temptations and perils faced by Elizabethan merchant–venturers is another example of how skilfully Shakespeare compels the association of ideas, this time by 'reverberation', that is, by echoing images from other parts of the play. Here we are invited to recall Salerio and Solanio's observations at the start of Act I, Scene i as well as Shylock's reference to 'the peril of waters, winds and rocks' (I.iii.25–6).

Lines 100–1 bring Bassanio's thoughts together and point the stereotyped Elizabethan moral about seeming and being. Thus Bassanio decides, not, as some critics suggest, to disregard the threatening inscription ('who chooseth me must give and hazard all he hath') but to take it into account when he makes his plunge. He is a gambler and has faith in the power of chance to make or mar a man. 'Joy' is ambiguous and in Middle and Early Modern English often implied erotic ecstasy.

Bassanio's final optimistic statement as he settles for the lead casket leads into Portia's 'aside' in rhymed couplets, a rare flash of intimacy on her part informing the audience what is passing through her mind, with her usual calculation absent. Her revealed response is spontaneous and contrasts with Bassanio's deliberate recitative. Rhyme is not basic to poetry nor essential to the couplet but here it suggests the orderliness associated with the mistress of Belmont, striving to keep an excess of emotion under the control of intellect. She apostrophises Love (*Eros* or *Cupid*, the deity of bodily desire) but, echoing Bassanio's word, prays for the 'joy' of Love's 'measure', that is, moderacy. The words 'measure' and 'blessing' prefigure the opening lines of her 'mercy' speech.

Aristotelian philosophy held that passion had to be controlled by reason. The Greek ideal, adopted by the Elizabethans, was balance (*temperantia*), midway between excess and deficiency. Portia is afraid that she may 'surfeit' (114) and fall a victim to the Deadly Sin of gluttony, normally associated with food. Christian authority, following St Thomas Aquinas, supported this doctrine and Portia seeks to act by it. Her pun on two meanings of 'fear' recalls the extravagant wordplay of *Love's Labour's Lost* and the earlier comedies. The adjectives applied to despair, fear and jealousy (110) each relate to iconographical conventions and the emblem books. According to the Thomist division despair and fear were two of the 'irascible' faculties, thought prone to provoke passion, while jealousy, another of the Seven Deadly Sins, was a species of hatred productive of disorder. Othello speaks of 'the green-eyed monster', a familiar metaphor.

7 CRITICAL RECEPTION

One of the joys of reading Shakespeare springs from the infinite variety of interpretations and judgements which his plays invite. He has a truly remarkable ability to make his audiences think about possible meanings and develop differing conclusions. This is particularly evident in the case of *The Merchant of Venice*.

The following examples show something of the range of critical opinion over the past century. Though his earliest admirers were sure that verisimilitude, or likeness to real life, was Shakespeare's aim, modern critics realise that nature may be mirrored in different ways. They are less concerned to applaud close conformity with actual human conduct than with asking what the stage action may convey without sacrificing artistic integrity.

What Shakespeare's original 'message' was cannot be known for certain, though it is unlikely that he had one specific intention in mind when he wrote *The Merchant*. Though few of the critics cited here would necessarily agree that this play was conceived as a denunciation of Elizabethan society, it does reveal just how unpleasant ordinary people may become if they find themselves confronted by an apparently alien entity which they see as a threat to their comfort and security. As such the characters and action transcend both place and time.

Of the authors quoted, John Masefield and W. H. Auden are poets, J. Russell Brown and Laurence Olivier practical men of the theatre, while the others are or have been university teachers. R. G. Moulton, whose first comment may be taken as a starting-point for study of *The Merchant*, was a distinguished scholar who taught in the United States.

The scene in which Bassanio makes his successful choice of the casket is the Dramatic centre of the whole play . . . it is the real crisis of the play . . . the apparent crisis is the Trial Scene, but this is in reality governed by the scene of the successful choice, and if

Portia and Bassanio had not been united in the earlier scene no lawyer would have interposed to turn the current of events in the trial. (R. G. Moulton, 1885)

The play resolves itself into a simple form. It illustrates the clash between the emotional and the intellectual characters, the man of heart and the man of brain. The man of heart, Antonio, is obsessed by a tenderness for his friend. The man of brain is obsessed by a lust to uphold intellect in a thoughtless world that makes intellect bitter in every age. (John Masefield, 1911)

We have seen that up to a certain point in Act 4 *The Merchant of Venice* moves towards Tragedy, and this movement is arrested only by Portia's challenge — 'Why doth the Jew pause?' By that challenge Antonio's life is saved . . . The Fifth Act redeems us into a world in which good folk are happy with free hearts that move to music, without an understanding of which a man is fit only for treasons, stratagems and spoils. (Arthur Quiller–Couch, 1926)

Shall we say it is a play about give and take – about conundrums such as the more you give, the more you get, or, to him that hath shall be given, and from him that hath not, shall be taken away even that which he hath? The two parts of the play are linked by these problems . . . in the scramble of give and take, where appearance and reality are hard to distinguish, one thing seems certain: that giving is the most important part – giving prodigally, without thought for the taking. (John Russell Brown, 1959)

Shylock, however unintentionally, did, in fact, hazard all for the sake of destroying the enemy he hated, and Antonio, however unthinkingly he signed the bond, hazarded all to secure the happiness of the friend he loved. Yet it is precisely these two who cannot enter Belmont. Belmont would like to believe that men and women are either good or bad by nature, but Shylock and Antonio remind us that this is an illusion: in the real world no hatred is totally without justification, no love totally innocent. (W. H. Auden, 1963)

The play performs convincingly: the stereotyped 'wicked Jew' of literature is perhaps no more offensive to Semites than the stereotyped 'wicked stepmother' of fairy stories is damaging to second wives. (Harry Blamires, 1974)

Shylock was probably intended to be received as an odious villain and a comic gull . . . If critics have differed as much as the actors about the interpretation of this character, it is not because he is enigmatic like Hamlet or profound like Iago or mysterious like Cleopatra, but because he is a man of 'confus'd', 'variable' passions and thus an odd mixture of incompatible traits. It is this curious medley, in which no passion can assimilate others, that makes him a comic character. (S. C. Sen Gupta, 1977)

That play seems to have come unstuck so early that Shakespeare more or less gave up trying to press it into a whole. He seems, even, to be contriving additional complications, to keep himself (and us?) from being bored with the ill-assorted box of tricks he has to work with. (John Wain, 1980)

In my time Shylock has been played with varying degrees of highly emotional sentimentality, the actors determined to wring from the trial scene a pulsating sense of nobility. I honestly feel this is pitching it a bit high. I find it impossible to think of Shylock as a really nice chap; he is just better-quality stuff than any of the Christians in the play. They are truly vile, heartless, money-grabbing monsters and when Shylock makes his final exit, destroyed by defeat, one should sense that our Christian brothers are at last thoroughly ashamed of themselves. *The Merchant of Venice* is horrid, cruel and one of the most popular plays in the whole collected volume. What is more it is thought to be eminently suitable for schoolchildren. (Laurence Olivier, 1986)

QUESTIONS

1. You have been briefed as Shylock's counsel. How would you defend him against the hostile opposition in the Duke's Court of law?
2. Justify the title *The Merchant of Venice* against the alternative *The Jew of Venice*. Can you suggest, and explain, a third?
3. Do you agree with those who find *The Merchant of Venice* eminently suitable for school production?
4. Does Act V of *The Merchant of Venice* represent a mastery of stagecraft or just a belated attempt by Shakespeare to shift the dramatic mood back to the comic? Argue for and/or against the policy of eighteenth-century producers who believed that the play was better without it.
5. Illustrate from the play Shakespeare's use of contrast, relating it to character and situation.
6. Portia, a splendid lady or a domineering pedant? Which of these nineteenth-century views do you prefer and how does it affect your opinion of the play as a whole?
7. Suggest two approaches to the portrayal of Jessica. How might the actor's portrayal of Lorenzo be thus affected?
8. Strong women and weak men. Is this a fair account of the types of lovers presented in *The Merchant of Venice*?
9. Show how Shakespeare suits language to character.
10. What do the minor characters contribute to our knowledge of the major characters?
11. Do you agree with those who think that *The Merchant of Venice* lacks unity?

APPENDIX:
SHAKESPEARE'S THEATRE
BY HAROLD BROOKS

We should speak, as Muriel Bradbrook reminds us, not of the Elizabethan stage but of Elizabethan stages. Plays of Shakespeare were acted on tour, in the halls of mansions, one at least in Gray's Inn, frequently at Court, and after 1609 at the Blackfriars, a small, roofed theatre for those who could afford the price. But even after his Company acquired the Blackfriars, we know of no play of his not acted (unless, rather improbably, *Troilus* is an exception) for the general public at the Globe, or before 1599 at its predecessor, The Theatre, which, since the Globe was constructed from the same timbers, must have resembled it. Describing the Globe, we can claim therefore to be describing, in an acceptable sense, Shakespeare's theatre, the physical structure his plays were designed to fit. Even in the few probably written for a first performance elsewhere, adaptability to that structure would be in his mind.

For the facilities of the Globe we have evidence from the drawing of the Swan theatre (based on a sketch made by a visitor to London about 1596) which depicts the interior of another public theatre; the builder's contract for the Fortune theatre, which in certain respects (fortunately including the dimensions and position of the stage) was to copy the Globe; indications in the dramatic texts; comments, like Ben Jonson's on the throne let down from above by machinery; and eye-witness testimony to the number of spectators (in round figures, 3000) accommodated in the auditorium.

In communicating with the audience, the actor was most favourably placed. Soliloquising at the centre of the front of the great platform, he was at the mid-point of the theatre, with no one among the spectators more than sixty feet away from him. That platform-stage (Figs I and II) was the most important feature for performance at the Globe. It had the audience – standing in the yard (10) and seated in the galleries (9) – on three sides of it. It was 43 feet wide, and $27^1/_2$ feet from front to back. Raised ($?5^1/_2$ feet) above the level of the yard, it had a trap-door (II.8) giving access to the space below it.

The actors, with their equipment, occupied the 'tiring house' (attiring-house: 2) immediately at the back of the stage. The stage-direction 'within' means inside the tiring-house. Along its frontage, probably from the top of the second storey, juts out the canopy or 'Heavens', carried on two large pillars rising through the platform (6, 7) and sheltering the rear part of the stage, the rest of which, like the yard, was open to the sky. If the 'hut' (I.8), housing the machinery for descents, stood, as in the Swan drawing, above the 'Heavens', that covering must have had a trap-door, so that the descents could be made through it.

Descents are one illustration of the vertical dimension the dramatist could use to supplement the playing-area of the great platform. The other opportunities are provided by the tiring-house frontage or facade. About this facade the evidence is not as complete or clear as we should like, so that Fig. I is in part conjectural. Two doors giving entry to the platform there certainly were (3). A third (4) is probable but not certain. When curtained, a door, most probably this one, would furnish what must be termed a discovery-space (II.5), not an inner stage (on which action in any depth would have been out of sight for a significant part of the audience). Usually no more than two actors were revealed (exceptionally, three) who often then moved out on to the platform. An example of this is Ferdinand and Miranda in *The Tempest* 'discovered' at chess, then seen on the platform speaking with their fathers. Similarly the gallery (I.5) was not an upper stage. Its use was not limited to the actors: sometimes it functioned as 'lords' rooms' for favoured spectators, sometimes, perhaps, as a musicians' gallery. Frequently the whole gallery would not be needed for what took place aloft: a window-stage (as in the first balcony scene in *Romeo*, even perhaps in the second) would suffice. Most probably this would be a part (at one end) of the gallery itself; or just possibly, if the gallery did not (as it does in the Swan drawing) extend the whole width of the tiring-house, a window over the left or right-hand door. As the texts show, whatever was presented aloft, or in the discovery-space, was directly related to the action on the platform, so that at no time was there left, between the audience and the action of the drama, a great bare space of platform-stage. In relating Shakespeare's drama to the physical conditions of the theatre, the primacy of that platform is never to be forgotten.

Note: The present brief account owes most to C. Walter Hodges, *The Globe Restored*; Richard Hosley in *A New Companion to Shakespeare Studies*, and in *The Revels History of English Drama*; and to articles by Hosley and Richard Southern in *Shakespeare Survey*, 12, 1959, where full discussion can be found.

HAROLD BROOKS

SHAKESPEARE'S THEATRE

The stage and its adjuncts; the tiring-house; and the auditorium.

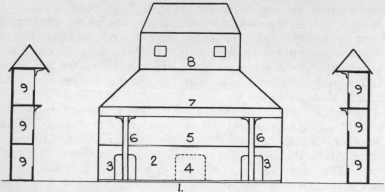

FIG I ELEVATION

1. Platform stage (approximately five feet above the ground) 2. Tiring-house
3. Tiring-house doors to stage 4. Conjectured third door 5. Tiring-house
gallery (balustrade and partitioning not shown) 6. Pillars supporting the
heavens 7. The heavens 8. The hut 9. The spectators' galleries

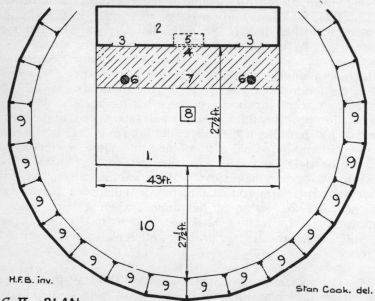

H.F.B. inv.

Stan Cook. del.

FIG II PLAN

1. Platform stage 2. Tiring-house 3. Tiring-house doors to stage
4. Conjectural third door 5. Conjectural discovery space (alternatively behind 3)
6. Pillars supporting the heavens 7. The heavens 8. Trap door 9. Spectators'
gallery 10. The yard

The Globe

An artist's imaginative recreation of a typical Elizabethan theatre

FURTHER READING

It should be emphasised (1) that 'further reading' is no substitute for a thorough and painstaking study of the text itself with the help of a reliable commentary and (2) that the finest intellectual resource for reading any Shakespeare play is the reader's imaginative ability to bring his own common sense to bear on the questions it suggests and not to expect the dramatist to furnish clear-cut answers. Though *The Merchant of Venice* was conceived as a play for stage performance it has also become a 'prescribed text' for examination purposes and the following short list of secondary sources has been drawn up to help the student preparing for examination.

Alexander, M., *Shakespeare and His Contemporaries* (Heinemann: Reader's Guide series, 1979).

Badawi, M.M., *Background to Shakespeare* (Macmillan, 1981) contains a short account of Shakespeare's use of classical myth.

Brown, J. R., (ed.), *The Merchant of Venice* (Arden edn: Methuen, 1977), introduction.

Brown, J. R., *Shakespeare and his Comedies* (Methuen, 1968), chapter 3, 'Love's Wealth and the Judgement of *The Merchant of Venice*'.

Brown, J. R., *Discovering Shakespeare, a New Guide to the Plays* (Macmillan, 1981).

Granville-Barker, H., *Prefaces to Shakespeare* (London, 1923–46: 4 vols); vol II refers to *The Merchant of Venice*.

Knight, G. Wilson, *Principles of Shakespearean Production* (Pelican Books, 1949), pp. 134–40 on 'an ideal production' of *The Merchant of Venice*.

Muir, K. and S. Schoenbaum, *A New Companion to Shakespeare Studies* (Cambridge, 1971).

Palmer, D. J., '*The Merchant of Venice* and the importance of being earnest', chapter V of *Shakespearean Comedy* (Stratford-Upon-Avon Studies No. 14: Arnold, 1972).

Powell, R., *Shakespeare and the Critics' Debate: a Guide For Students* (Macmillan, 1968).

Stephen, M. and Philip Franks, *Studying Shakespeare* (Longman: York Handbooks, 1984).

Stevens, P., *Shakespeare and His Theatre* (Wayland Publications, 1973).

Wilders, J. (ed.), *The Merchant of Venice: a Casebook* (Macmillan, 1969) contains fifteen recent essays and a select bibliography.